A Ford,
not a
Lincoln

A Ford, not a Lincoln

Richard Reeves

HBJ Harcourt Brace Jovanovich New York and London

Library of Congress Cataloging in Publication Data

Reeves, Richard.
 A Ford, not a Lincoln.

 Includes index.
 1. Ford, Gerald R., 1913-   I.   Title.
E866.R46   973.925′092′4 [B]   75-22195
ISBN 0-15-132302-X

First edition

B C D E

To Mag   To Cindie and Jeff

Contents

Introduction

Jerry Ford is a pretty nice guy and a professional politician. This book is about the latter. Specifically, it is about his first hundred days as President of the United States. It is also, I hope, about what I've learned about American politics and leadership in ten years as a newspaper reporter and magazine writer.

Writing about an incumbent President is an interesting experience, to say the least, because many people are afraid of the enormous power centered in the White House. Some just wouldn't talk. Some lied. Most, especially practicing politicians, told part of the truth. But more than 150 men and women did talk to me at some length after I began writing about Ford a year ago and as I became more interested in what I saw—a rather ordinary man in extraordinary circumstances.

I do have a bias in writing about politicians. I don't feel any great obligation to recount their many and varied personal and professional virtues. That is what they, or the taxpayers, are paying for in the salaries and fees of press secretaries, media advisers, and advertising agencies. Believe me, there is nothing good about Jerry Ford, Nelson Rockefeller or any of the Kennedys that the American people have not been told—those politicians and all the others have staffs that make sure we know they love their country, wives, children, dogs and fellow man. As I was looking over this manuscript and wondering whether I was unfair to President Ford, the White House announced that he shot an 86 playing golf in Palm Springs. It was the first time his score was announced—I assume because it was the first time his score was that good. Parts of this book are about days when his score wasn't very good and wasn't announced.

. . .

I am grateful to the people who talked to me and in deep debt to those who were open and candid, even though many of their names do not appear in the book at their request. I also have the usual list of the people who, for better or worse, made me what I am today, beginning with my mother, Dorothy Reeves, who thought it was nice to have a son who was a $90-a-week reporter instead of a $300-a-week mechanical engineer. And Carol Reeves. Then there are the men who gave me the spastic colon, editors all, merciless and good: Clay Felker of *New York* magazine, Lewis Bergman of the New York *Times Magazine,* Artie Gelb and Abe Rosenthal and Shelly Binn of the New York *Times,* and Danny Blum, now of the *Times,* but in my memory saying through his cigar stub on the city desk of the New York *Herald Tribune,* "You'll do, kid!"

And, on this book, there were Lynn Nesbit, my agent, who waited eight years for me to do it, and Tony Godwin, my editor, a man who knows the difference between words and writing. There were also friends who gave their time and talent to protect me from my own failings, especially Ken Auletta, Steve Weisman and Amanda Urban. And Bob Woodward, Dick Cohen, Robert Peabody, Robert Sherrill, Sheilah Koeppen, Eugene Kennedy and Jean Kidd. Also Mary Ellen Leary and Ed Salzman of the *California Journal* and Robert Goldmann of the Ford Foundation, who

x

helped me more than I helped them as an adviser to the *Journal's* study of candidate-media interaction in the California elections of 1974. Alex Craig, a Drew University student, was my researcher, and without him I'd still be working.

The opinions and mistakes, as they say, are mine, all mine.

Richard Reeves

Washington, D.C.
April 1975

1

The Man Without Enemies

"Fiercer far than the light which beats upon a throne is the light which beats upon a presidential candidate, searching out all the recesses of his past life. Hence, when the choice is between a brilliant man and a safe man, the safe man is preferred."

James B. Bryce,
The American Commonwealth, 1888

ON THE DAY after New Year's 1963, two of the younger and brighter Republican members of the U.S. House of Representatives met for lunch and did what younger congressmen often do—they griped. Charles Goodell, 36, of New York, and Robert Griffin, 39, of Michigan, griped mainly about their leader, 63-year-old House Minority Leader Charles Halleck, who thought young Republican congressmen should be neither seen nor heard very much. But with just ten years of seniority between them, there wasn't much Goodell and Griffin could do about old Charlie Halleck.

"What if we went after Hoeven?" Goodell said.

Charles Hoeven of Iowa was 67, and he was the chairman of the House Republican Conference; on paper he was the number three man in the party leadership, but actually he didn't do much of anything—Hoeven had called only one conference meeting in two years. The two rebels—they would soon be called the Young Turks—made up a list of five younger men who might challenge Hoeven in the caucus of 178 Republican House members. The first four men on the list said no, they were not interested in symbolic challenges. The fifth name was Ford—Gerald R. Ford, Jr., 49, representative of the Fifth District of Michigan since 1949. He said yes, and in a secret caucus ballot the vote was Ford, 86, Hoeven, 78.

"It wasn't as though everybody was wildly enthusiastic about Jerry," Goodell said. "It was just that most Republicans liked and respected him. He didn't have enemies."

It hardly seemed a momentous event in American politics. The little rebellion rated just one paragraph in most newspapers, usually quoting Hoeven as saying, "I was picked as the lamb for slaughter." Jerry Ford was, by vote of his peers, a leader.

Characteristically, Ford avoided offending anyone during his two years as conference chairman; like Hoeven, he rarely convened the conference to discuss party policy or strategy.

Halleck, meanwhile, continued to rub people the wrong way—he was a determined, energetic leader, but he rarely consulted his troops, and one of them characterized his attitude as "detached arrogance." Came November 1964, and Barry Goldwater's disastrous loss to President Johnson, along with the loss of thirty-eight Republican House seats. It was clearly time for a change—and time for Goodell and Griffin to have lunch again.

This time, November 25, 1964, the two seasoned rebels were joined by four other restive young Republicans— Thomas Curtis of Missouri, Albert Quie of Minnesota, and Donald Rumsfeld and John Anderson of Illinois. The six original conspirators and two dozen others who later joined them considered only two choices to challenge Halleck: Ford, the favorite because he was already a member of the leadership as conference chairman, and Melvin Laird of Wisconsin. The decision was fairly easy, one of the young congressmen said, at the time:

"Laird is more controversial. He's more dynamic. He's got more leadership. At the same time, he's irritated and antagonized some people, made enemies along the line. Ford has not. I don't know how you measure these things. It's a feeling, a reading you get. There were fewer people mad at Ford . . ."

On December 17, Goodell, Griffin and Quie informed the

6

man without enemies that he was the Young Turk choice. Ford begged off for a couple of days, saying he wanted to talk with his family and a personal circle of advisers, mainly business types, executives of the automobile companies, U.S. Steel, the National Association of Manufacturers and the U.S. Chamber of Commerce. The theme of the Ford campaign, announced December 19, was "better communication of the Republican message through new techniques and bold leadership." Hardly a ringing battle cry, their theme deliberately emphasized public relations over public policy. The new technique, Ford's supporters explained, was television, and their man looked a lot bolder on it than grumpy old Charlie Halleck. Besides, Ford, at the urging of Goodell and Griffin, was taking lessons from a voice coach.

There was no overriding ideological issue in the contest. Both Halleck and Ford were to the right of the center of the Republican party; older conservatives and liberals tended to vote for Halleck, and younger conservatives and liberals tended to vote for Ford. The younger man won by a secret caucus vote of 73 to 67, and rather than promising to lead, he pledged himself as a "team player," one of his favorite phrases.*

Ford's behavior during their coup mystified and sometimes irritated Goodell and Griffin. Their candidate took three separate vacations between Thanksgiving and New Year's— sunning in Puerto Rico, golfing in Palm Springs and skiing

---

* Halleck, Ford and Laird were judged equally conservative—and more conservative than their Republican House colleagues—by Robert L. Peabody of the Johns Hopkins University. Professor Peabody rated Republican representatives in the 89th Congress on a scale of "0" (most conservative) to "18" (most liberal), based on eighteen roll call votes on "Federal role support." Halleck, Ford and Laird were rated at "5," compared with a Republican average of "7" and a Democratic average of "13." Professor Peabody's study of the Halleck-Ford contest will be published in 1976 by Little, Brown (Boston) under the title *Leadership in Congress: Stability, Succession and Change.*

in Michigan before the defeat of Halleck on January 4. One night, the two campaign managers plotted to keep Ford in his office telephoning congressmen for support by bringing him sandwiches and Cokes and persuading him the food would be wasted if he went home for dinner. It was not that Ford was lazy or without ambition—he had very much wanted to be Barry Goldwater's running mate for Vice-President the summer before—but it was not his style to get actively engaged in a fight. You can lose friends that way.

"I did it because I had nothing to lose," Ford told me almost ten years later. "I could have kept my House seat, and I was careful not to get anyone mad at me."

But he won. Jerry Ford, quite suddenly it seemed, was a major factor in American government. Newspapers and magazines were taken aback by Halleck's defeat and were not quite sure what to make of the new minority leader, except to repeatedly label him, as did the New York *Times*, Washington *Post* and *Time* magazine, "a former football star" and "a hard-working member of the Appropriations Committee." (Ford, at six feet and 197 pounds, was the second-string center on the University of Michigan's national champion teams in 1932 and 1933; in 1934, he was a starter and the team's most valuable player, but Michigan lost seven of its eight games.)

There were, however, a couple of interesting bits of reporting about the new leader. "Ford," wrote Julius Duscha of the *Post,* "is lean, well-tailored, repectably conservative, never too far ahead of the country club crowd. He would have done as well at General Motors as he has on Capitol Hill." *The Reporter* magazine said: "Ford was not a particularly popular choice. The young conservatives who promoted him really would have preferred the more aggressive Melvin Laird, who moved into Ford's old job as conference chairman. Similarly, his liberal backers were disappointed that they didn't have the chance to support someone less conservative."

The Reporter had it only slightly wrong. In fact, Ford was

8

not a particularly unpopular choice. The congressman from Grand Rapids was the least objectionable alternative. He brought to mind James B. Bryce's words in *The American Commonwealth* in 1888:

"The methods and habits of Congress and indeed of political life generally, seem to give fewer opportunities for personal distinction, fewer modes in which a man may commend himself to his countrymen by eminent capacity in thought, in speech or in administration . . . Eminent men make more enemies, and give those enemies more assailable points, than obscure men do. They are therefore in so far less desirable candidates."

Lord Bryce's models were some of the United States' most undistinguished nineteenth-century Presidents: "The only thing remarkable about them is that being so commonplace they should have climbed so high." His judgments were not dissimilar to the off-the-record quotes of some of the Republicans who had just elevated Gerald Ford to leadership.

ELEVEN YEARS after Goodell and Griffin put him fifth on their little list, Gerald R. Ford became the President of the United States.

Bill Moyers, writing in *Newsweek,* commented on that extraordinary event by conducting a fantasy interview with Alexis de Tocqueville, who wrote the classic *Democracy in America* after touring the new United States in the 1830's:

" 'Gerald Ford spent his whole career in Congress proving that he could not possibly be President,' Tocqueville said, 'and look where he is now.'

" 'He's an exception—a fluke,' Moyers answered.

" 'Politics in your country is the triumph of the flukes,' Tocqueville said with a sigh."

Ford may have become President by accident, but it was no accident that a Ford became President. In many ways he was the very model of a modern American politician. His success was a triumph of lowest-common-denominator politics, the survival of the man without enemies, the least objectionable alternative. The remarkable thing about Ford and others like him is that they have won leadership by carefully avoiding it. The act and art of leading inevitably offends and alienates some of the people some of the time in a democratic universe,

11

as Charlie Halleck discovered. His successor, Gerald Ford, built his career and life on avoiding offending anyone. Ford's discovery, shared by many in modern America, was no small thing. It was that the highest national honors and rewards could be won by limiting oneself to commonplace virtues—ambition, perseverance and caution.

There is nothing wrong with ambition in America. It's as American as Horatio Alger, and a man obviously does not become President—or minority leader of the House—without being ambitious. Jerry Ford got where he did because he wanted to and worked like hell at it; our candidates, and thus our governors, are self-selected and self-promoted. No one persuaded Ford to run for Congress when he came home from the Navy after World War II. The path to the White House began when he told his friends at South High School in Grand Rapids that he wanted to be a congressman. He was on his way when he told his new wife in 1948 that his fourteen-hour work-days and perseverance might someday make him Speaker of the House. The hard glow of political ambition shows—it shows itself at places like the tennis court at the Washington Hilton Hotel at seven o'clock in the morning when two writers and another U.S. senator come upon Senator Lloyd Bentsen of Texas sitting alone in his whites, looking up surprised and saying the first thing that comes to mind: "Boy, I sure would like to be President!"

Congressmen, because they run for office every two years, are our distilled politicians. Running for office, not making laws or debating the issues of the day, is what they do for a living. They are professional candidates. But if congressmen do more campaigning, the difference between them and other professional public office seekers is only a matter of degree. Nelson Rockefeller, who was to become Ford's Vice-President, had enormous power and responsibility as governor of New York for fifteen years. In 1970 at the Pulaski Day Parade in Buffalo, he happened to meet a young man he had seen before at the St. Patrick's Day Parade in New York City; the young

12

man, Sandy Frucher, who was working for Rockefeller's opponent, Arthur Goldberg, said, "Governor, we seem to meet only at parades." Rockefeller answered with a wink, but perhaps with more truth than he usually does: "Son, parades are my business!"

Campaigning, too, is the business of Senator Thomas Eagleton of Missouri, one of the young men in American politics who succeeded by holding each of his public offices for as short a time as possible and doing as little as possible. Politics is one of the few businesses where accomplishment is measured by how often one changes jobs. In sixteen years, Tom Eagleton went from county circuit attorney to state attorney general to lieutenant governor to U.S. senator to Democratic nominee for Vice-President.

When it became known that his climbing was periodically interrupted by emotional problems, Eagleton talked about his first secret hospitalization after being elected attorney general of Missouri in 1960: "There's a letdown mood after an election. I guess it's like the closing night of a show. It's been a huge success, let's say, and it's the last night and there's a terrific letdown. You go from frenetic activity to *nothing* . . . there isn't very much to do. There aren't any more speeches to give, there aren't any more airplanes to catch. So you sit around and this mood of depression comes on."

Nothing, in Eagleton's business, was being the chief law enforcement officer of a state of five million people. Campaigning, now that's something—mind-numbing and superficial to most observers, "interpersonal aggression" in the phrase of political scientist James David Barber, but plasma to most politicians.

Outsiders, observers like reporters and political scientists, have trouble understanding the pull of campaigning for most politicians, probably because it cannot be understood—it must be felt. I have seen Ford, a 61-year-old man, shout, "Let's go!" as color and life came back into his face after seventeen hours of campaigning when an aide told him at 11 P.M. that there

13

was another Republican dinner he could still make that night. Robert Redford, who gets his share of adulation as an actor, told me he had never experienced anything like the overwhelming sense of power he felt when he pretended to be a senatorial candidate in an unannounced motorcade through the business district of San Francisco. "The people on the street didn't know who I was," he said, during the filming of *The Candidate*. "We just came in with loudspeakers and signs as if it were a real campaign. They were just giving themselves completely to the man waving on the back of a convertible."

And it does not have to be a man.

In a study of fifty women state legislators for the Center for the American Woman and Politics, Jeane J. Kirkpatrick of Georgetown University found that forty of them enjoyed campaigning to the point that the phrase "I love it!" became boringly redundant. "The campaign trail," she wrote, "more nearly resembles an endless series of club meetings than a duel . . . Smiles, speeches, favors, explanations, congratulations, ingratiation, deference, are the 'weapons' with which a candidate 'fights' . . . Probably the most important subjective requisite of effective campaigning is the capacity to enjoy it . . . Campaigning gives them the chance to seek and receive attention—all in a worthy cause."

Even the few politicians who do not like campaigning keep at it endlessly. Perseverance is as American as the McDonald's hamburger—and the success of the Big Mac is not unrelated to the ascendancy of Gerald Ford, or Richard Nixon, or Hubert Humphrey, or Nelson Rockefeller. All are proud men, but politicians' pride is not the kind that keeps them from trying and trying again.

Without ever being called pushy, Jerry Ford has always pressed on. It took six years of his life to get a degree from Yale Law School after he was told a football player from the University of Michigan could never make it there. He did make it, sitting in on classes without receiving credit before he was allowed to matriculate, taking summer law courses back at

14

Michigan, coaching the football and boxing teams, working as a male model and even selling as much as $25 worth of his blood a week as a professional donor.

McDonald's, the enormously successful institutionalization of American lowest-common-denominator marketing, would have loved young Jerry Ford, who certainly met the hamburger chain's training manual demands for "all-American boys . . . sincerity, enthusiasm, confidence." In fact, Ray Kroc, the founder and chairman of McDonald's, loves old Jerry Ford; at least he contributes hundreds of thousands of dollars to Republican campaigns. Kroc's favorite saying, "Press On," is displayed above the desks of McDonald's executives in framed scrolls with this inspirational message:

Nothing in the world can take the place of persistence.
Talent will not; nothing is more common than unsuccessful men with talent.
Genius will not; unrewarded genius is almost a proverb.
Education will not; the world is full of educated derelicts.
Persistence and determination alone are omnipotent.

McDonald's training manuals, it happens, read like a parody of modern least-objectionable-alternative politics. These are the instructions for McDonald's managers in college towns:

"Talk to the students in a direct manner. They call it 'talking straight.' Don't attempt to imitate what you think is their language and don't 'put them on.' They would say 'tell it like it is.' Be aware of local problems, especially campus problems, but avoid taking sides and steer clear of controversial areas. Don't jeopardize your restaurant's position as 'neutral ground.' "

That kind of creative caution is as American as Congress— in fact, if caution were an art, Capitol Hill would be the Louvre. "Congress, it seems to me, exists in a force field, like an electromagnetic field; it's hard to explain unless you've been there and felt it," said Wes Vivian, a professor of engineering at the University of Michigan, who was on Capitol Hill from 1965 to 1967 as a Democratic representative. "You

15

can't say what you think. Almost nobody in Congress says what he believes. How can you, when you know all the words you say may come back to haunt you. If you're in a marginal district, you can't afford to offend any group, any part of your constituency . . . The people there aren't as bad as I thought they would be—a third are pretty good, really good; there are 10 to 15 per cent who are comic, so bad they're outside discussion, and most are kind of neuter, they just fill up the seats. It's not that the neuter ones don't have the skills. They decided at some point not to use them. Congress is a personality-forming world and they're just there, inoffensive."

Ford, in Vivian's not unfriendly estimation, was near the top of the inoffensive group. "He had a great deal of freedom because he was from a safe district," Vivian said. "There's an old saying that if you get more than 55 per cent of the vote back home, you haven't used your potential—you could have offended more of your voters. Ford used his freedom in a different way because he wanted to be in the leadership. That's a very different thing from voting for things that might cause trouble but won't cost your seat—getting ahead internally depends on not offending anyone, avoiding entanglements, particularly ideological entanglements. You go to the gym, to the parties, you don't make enemies—it's a legitimate role inside the institution."

Members of Congress, of both the House and the Senate, are in many ways the worst that American politics can produce. Their career life style—maximizing comment and minimizing responsibility—occasionally leads to frustrated and cutting self-analysis like the private words of Representative Sam Steiger, an Arizona Republican: "Being a member of Congress is 90 per cent form—you get attention, you view with alarm, you offer no solutions." Congressional debate, for instance, is a farce, a comical imitation of what the men who wrote the Constitution must have had in mind a couple of hundred years ago. Even using the word "debate" is a bit farcical, unless it has been redefined to include dramatic gesturing at empty

16

desks and glancing at the Press Gallery to see whether the New York *Times* or Washington *Post* is taking notes. The elders, like grandees trailed by attendant entourages, wander from cameo appearances at committee hearings to National Airport for a quick flight, to a $2,500 college speech or an appearance back home to dazzle the folks with the glamour that has attached to them since the television networks decided Washington was America. Capitol Hill is America only if we have become a nation accustomed to deference, doormen, drivers, devoted secretaries, determined aides and Capitol policemen who stop traffic whenever a member is crossing the street.

"Washington," in words written by Arthur Hoppe in the San Francisco *Chronicle*, "is several miles square and about as tall, say, as the Washington Monument, give or take a little. It is surrounded on all four sides by reality." And Washington is where the great majority of American politicians stay if they retire or are defeated at home. They become Capitol lawyers, lobbyists, or bureaucrats. Like Thomas Wolfe, they can't go home again.

Ford was known as a "congressman's congressman." The description, meant as flattering and institutionalized one year in a plaque from the American Political Science Association, was essentially accurate—among other things, Ford was making as many as 238 out-of-town speeches a year, out of Washington and out of Grand Rapids. Like many senior members, he no longer represented his district as much as he represented his own leadership ambitions—even if any Grand Rapids resident could count on Ford's staff to work out personal problems with the Federal government.

Any congressman is capable of making his voting record look like all things to all men. Amendments, motions to recommit and other parliamentary parlor tricks make it possible for a Representative Ford to assert that he voted for final passage of every major civil rights bill during his tenure. Or he can let people know that up until the final votes, he fought to block every piece of civil rights legislation. He did

17

both, getting caught only once, when Grand Rapids newspapers accused him of working to kill fair-housing legislation in 1965, then voting for it when passage was inevitable.

Whatever Ford's deepest feelings were about civil rights—and friends said he had no deep feelings either way—he was able and willing to use that issue and others to trade for the valuable status of having no enemies in his own party. He kept the good will of conservative Republicans opposed to civil rights measures and of party liberals favoring those laws.

He was a certain type of leader—an accommodator. Ford was never a political compromiser in the sense of actively forging a party position out of divergent views. Rather, he allowed others, activists like Laird and Goodell, to try to build support for their positions. Then, and only then, Ford would accommodate himself to the compromise already worked out. He developed a certain genius for positioning himself just on the edge of the scene in his climb—it was no accident that Goodell and Griffin had trouble forcing him to stay on the scene in his own leadership fight—but he was always there to finally argue for the least objectionable alternative, or to be that alternative himself.

The term "least objectionable alternative" is adapted from another business, one that has been an important factor in molding new American politicians—television. Paul Klein, a former programming vice-president of the National Broadcasting Company, has used the phrase to discuss theories of television programming:

"The point of nearly every strategy and tactic of a network is to get the largest possible share of that audience in each half-hour . . . I call it the theory of The Least Objectionable Program . . . You view television irrespective of the content of the program watched . . . you take what is fed to you because you are compelled to exercise the medium.

"A very old law has also become more and more useful in figuring out program popularity. I mean the First Law of Motion, the one that says a body at rest tends to stay at rest.

18

Once a viewer chooses his LOP, he may have to fiddle with a lot of knobs should he decide to switch channels.

"The best network programmers understand this. They are not stupid. They know a program doesn't have to be 'good.' It only has to be less objectionable than whatever the hell the other guys throw against it."

And the people who run our lives and country are not that stupid either. Many of them have figured out that the incredible reach of television has made coalition-building and the kind of leadership it took to build those coalitions a thing of the past. Going right into living rooms with situation comedies and cop shows, modern politicians can survive as long as they don't offend large numbers of voters. You don't have to like them or follow them as long as you don't get aggravated enough to take the energy to switch channels.

Many of the new generation of "leaders" are not slaves of public opinion polls, as they are sometimes represented, and they are not trying to tell people what they want to hear. Rather, they are avoiding telling people what they don't want to hear. Refined political pragmatists are not afraid to oppose popular programs if a significant minority of voters are against those programs. The voters to watch out for are aroused negative voters. Most politicians, particularly incumbents, have nothing against apathy, boredom or disdain among the electorate. They don't need enthusiasm; what can kill them is an excited minority.

The survival of George Wallace as a major political force is a case in point. Over the past few years I have talked with almost every other Presidential-class American politician about the Alabama governor, and their assessments of him are just about identical. He is, in their minds, an ignorant and dangerous demagogue playing on the fears and darkest impulses of a segment of the nation. But even though national polls indicated that as many as two-thirds of the American people were strongly anti-Wallace, those judgments stayed locked inside the minds of Humphrey, the Kennedys, Mc-

19

Govern, Rockefeller. They said nothing—even when Wallace's national support was at only about 10 per cent and their united voices might have destroyed him. The inertial two-thirds was not their problem; they were afraid of an aroused 10 per cent.

A mark of modern political technicians, the campaign managers, is that they have come to understand that elections today are not so much a contest between opponents as a contest first for access to the media, particularly television, and then for effective use of the media. In California in 1974, the governorship was won by Edmund G. (Jerry) Brown, Jr., who had access to media because of his name—his father was a former governor—and because he already held public office, secretary of state. The Brown strategy, as explained *after the election* by his 30-year-old manager, Thomas Quinn, was: "We didn't want to offend or excite anyone. We were ahead so we wanted a dull, dull, dull campaign. We found obscure, boring issues and talked about them—Jerry's real ideas were dangerous, but we were generally successful in avoiding them. It was sometimes hard to restrain him because he is essentially an activist. But obviously we were successful, we won."

Brown's campaign slogan, "A New Spirit," was creatively meaningless, as is a great deal of modern political rhetoric. Perhaps, when a candidate is as young as Jerry Brown, he has to restrain himself to master the art of speech without substance or offense, but with practice the conditioning becomes the condition—leaders incapable of leadership. One of the essential techniques for television campaigning—John F. Kennedy was an early master—is the art of talking about public problems without commitment to any solutions. It is solutions that make people mad, so the modern candidate defines and deplores the problem—many like to refer to themselves as nonideological "problem solvers" because no voter is against solving problems—and promises we can do better. He shows that he cares and then talks about the future, preferably the far future.

20

Or the candidate can talk about the past—it's almost as safe as the far future. What does the slogan "Come Home, America" mean? I don't know, and I don't think John Lindsay, Edmund Muskie or George McGovern knew, or cared, when they used it in their 1972 Presidential campaigns. It was creatively meaningless, and the reason all three used the same slogan at different times was that its creator—a bright young speech writer named Robert Schrum—moved successively from Lindsay's staff to Muskie's, then to McGovern's.

Like their slogans, politicians tend to sound better, more profound, than they actually are. These are quick people, their intelligence is like an oil slick, always spreading and usually about as deep. You can say, "He has a short attention span," or "He's a quick study," or "He has a great instinct for getting right to the heart of the matter, for asking the right questions" —the normal description of politicians may be unkind or kind, but the three phrases mean essentially the same thing.

Or as Charles Coy, the Republican state chairman of Kentucky, told me about Ronald Reagan in 1973: "We sure do like him down here. But as my daddy used to say, 'Some men are as thin as piss on a slate rock.' " Anyway, this is what three pretty bright modern politicians sound like in action:

Senator Jacob Javits of New York dodging questions on Watergate and the scandals of Richard Nixon: "It's dismaying. It would be pointless of me to blame it on anybody. The point is to look forward . . ."

Senator Edward Kennedy of Massachusetts tackling the energy crisis by storming into his office and snapping at the staff: "Get me an energy program by next week—I'm sick of Scoop Jackson being called 'Mr. Energy.' "

Then there was Senator George McGovern running for the Democratic nomination for President in 1972 by touring the Massachusetts Correctional Institution at Concord—a typical media-attracting event. He walked through the yard with the warden, James O'Shea, and their conversation was questions and answers: How many men do you have in here? Six hundred and seventy-eight; the capacity, though, is 550. What would be the ideal size for a prison like this? One hundred men, 150 tops.

When the tour was over and the television lights went on, McGovern had a crisp opening statement: "There are more than 600 men here in an institution designed for only 550. Now, I believe that the ideal maximum capacity for an institution like this is 150—one hundred would be even better. I think the superintendent here would readily agree." O'Shea blinked and nodded dumbly as the television lights swung toward his face.

Politicians are different from you and me. The business of accumulating power over people does something to a man or woman—even when that man is reluctant to use the power because using it brings responsibility and risk. He closes himself off from other men until he reaches the point where he instinctively calculates each new situation and each other person with the simplest question: What can this do for me or to me? The process seems as inevitable and as frightening as hardening of the arteries. It is not unusual for political journalists, the outsiders who often get closest to politicians, to develop views of them like the one expressed a couple of years ago by the English journalist Auberon Waugh: "It is my settled opinion, after some years as a political correspondent, that no one is attracted to a political career in the first place unless he is socially or emotionally crippled."

There is a substantial literature, much of which can be traced back to Erik Erikson and Harold Laswell, the great University of Chicago political scientist, contending that persons who seek public power are essentially seeking to compensate for feelings of personal insecurity. Undoubtedly there is a great deal of truth to that, but my own experience, after some years as a political correspondent, has given me the settled opinion that the political process itself molds a certain kind of political man or woman. The politician, for instance, will usually tell you that his greatest strength is "getting along

22

with people"—a euphemism for not making enemies. In fact, however, most politicians seem to have a guarded contempt for the people they get along with, represent and lead, or pretend to lead.

People, when you see too many of them for the briefest and most artificial moments, when too many of them want something from you, become so many objects to be quickly stroked and manipulated. The communication of politics becomes a series of conditioned moves—the speech of American clichés, the hearty laugh, the wave, the slap on the back, the fondled bicep, "Hi, howareya? Good to see you!"

Congressman Jerome Waldie was another Democrat in the 1974 campaign for governor of California. He had no inherited access to the media, so he walked the 1,000 miles from the bottom to the top of the state to try to attract television cameras. His comments on the experience revealed more about his relationship to "the people" than he realized:

"I love this . . . In all my years in politics, I've done what politicians do, talk to people in the power centers. This is different. I see people who have never seen a politician in their lives . . . on the street, for that twenty seconds I'm shaking his hands and looking at him and saying, 'Hi, I'm Jerry Waldie. What's your name?' That is more honest and direct communication than the voter ever gets . . ."

Only a professional would think twenty seconds was meaningful human communication. But Jerry Ford had figured it out years before Jerry Waldie. In the corner of Ford's Capitol office, there was a Polaroid camera permanently mounted on a tripod facing his desk for the purpose of taking an endless series of ten-second photographs showing him shaking hands with constituents visiting Washington or, if he was not around, of constituents sitting in his big, red chair. When they left the office the folks were handed a bumper sticker that said "We visited Congressman Jerry Ford."

That is what politicians usually mean when they say, "I've been talking with the people"—and I have heard Gerald Ford use that phrase a dozen times after shaking chains of hands at receptions.

"A politician's words reveal less about what he thinks about his subject than what he thinks about his audience," wrote columnist George F. Will, commenting about a brief statement in *Harper's* magazine by Ronald Reagan in March 1975. The former California governor was one of a number of politicians asked to answer the question, "When did you stop wanting to be President?" Reagan's answer began, "I never started," which prompted Will to write: "He thinks America has suffered amnesia. But America has etched on its mental retina the image of Reagan, a declared candidate at the 1968 Republican Convention, fighting skillfully and tenaciously for the nomination . . . To be fair, I'm sure Reagan didn't mean what he wrote. Alas, being fair to politicians often involves pleading them guilty to lesser charges."

GERALD FORD, the minority leader was always something of a joke in Washington. But the Ford jokes usually had a touch of affection in them. He was, after all, a nice guy, and beyond that there was the feeling that if you were drowning, Jerry Ford would jump in after you. That is a rare quality in a city where most men would publicly comfort your widow and introduce tough new water safety legislation.

The jokes were about Ford's brains—or lack of same. President Johnson, in tired legend, was the source of the most repeated, about playing football too long without a helmet, and "Jerry Ford is so dumb he can't walk and chew gum at the same time." * Then there was the time the minority leader was opposing the President's Model Cities legislation and Johnson told one of his assistants, "Joe, you've got a little baby boy. Well, you take his little building blocks and go up and explain to Jerry Ford what we're trying to do."

Ford, a good-humored man without any particular sense of humor, always pretended that he didn't mind the jokes. But of course he did, and he sometimes reacted by telling people

* What Johnson actually said was, "Jerry Ford is so dumb he can't fart and chew gum at the same time." The late President's aides and history have cleaned up the remark.

that he graduated in the top third of his class at South High School in Grand Rapids and at the University of Michigan and at Yale Law School. Without knowing the lower two-thirds of South High's class of '31, it is fair to say that Ford is slow. He is also unimaginative and not very articulate.

"Johnson thought Ford was stupid because he was predictable—he could maneuver around Jerry," said his friend Charlie Goodell. "Ford is a solid, inertial guy. He is genuinely naïve, and he has no instinct for power, for manipulation . . . It took him a year or two to adjust to being minority leader. He continued to act as if he were still just a congressman from Grand Rapids."

The congressman from Grand Rapids, however, was being treated as a national leader, and as Goldwater supporters had complained about reporters in 1964, there were people out there writing down everything he said. Because of Ford's new title, what he said was suddenly news—even his campaign in the spring of 1966 to persuade the House Space Committee or Armed Services Committee to investigate reports of unidentified flying objects in Michigan. When the Air Force sent in investigators who reported that the sightings were swamp gas and clever college boys using flares to impress the girls at Hillsdale College, Ford rebutted that he still wanted a congressional investigation because "it would make people feel better." And when the rest of Congress still said no, the minority leader had one more shot: "There are people who ridicule my call for a congressional investigation of UFO's but my mail is overwhelmingly in favor of my stand."

If substituting mail counts for judgment was fatuous, Ford was as willing to play games with larger issues. In a 1966 economic double reverse that he would repeat on a larger stage nine years later as President, Ford managed to get on three sides of the same question within twelve days.

On April 22 of that year, Minority Leader Ford called a press conference to denounce "Johnson Inflation" and asked when the President would "apply the brakes."

26

On the morning of May 3, Ford saw a report that automobile sales were down in the first two weeks of April and issued a statement attacking Johnson, saying the President "has applied the brakes too hard, and this may throw the economy into a tailspin." When he was asked what brakes the President had applied, Ford said he was referring to the effects of higher interest rates ordered by the Federal Reserve Board. The Board, which is independent, had indeed raised interest rates, but that had been five months earlier, and Johnson had vehemently objected.

But there was more to come—on the afternoon of May 3, General Motors, Chrysler and Ford Motor all announced that their sales hit a record high in the *last* two weeks of April. The next day Ford attacked "Johnson Inflation."

Politicians might argue that shoveling smoke at the opposition is a legitimate partisan function of any minority leader, but Ford's judgment was also suspect in the inner circles of his own party. Richard J. Whalen, a speech writer for Richard Nixon in the 1968 campaign, remembers Ford's contribution to a Vietnam strategy discussion: "I listened in disbelief one morning as House Minority Leader Gerald Ford earnestly told a breakfast gathering that the answer to Tet was to. *Americanize* the war effort."

If Ford's advice was sometimes ignored, his loyalty to the party and all its members never was—unbending, undying, unthinking loyalty. When the Senate voted not to confirm President Richard Nixon's appointment of G. Harrold Carswell to the Supreme Court, Ford loyally and foolishly acted as the President's tool of vengeance. With the help of a friendly young lawyer named Benton Becker, the minority leader collected a garbage can of files from the office of Attorney General John Mitchell and tried to make a case for the impeachment of Supreme Court Justice William O. Douglas. He saw things like that as part of the job, once telling friends that John Anderson of Illinois would be the best choice to succeed him as minority leader, except that Anderson had a flaw:

27

"He's the smartest guy in Congress, but he insists on voting his conscience instead of party."

Ford's devotion to party and Nixon also led him to lie— or at least consciously deceive—on the floor of the House. He was one of the handful of congressional leaders who had been informed of secret American bombing of neutral Cambodia for two years before the 1970 incursion by South Vietnamese troops. Then, on November 16, 1970, after the South Vietnamese action, when Nixon said that the United States had scrupulously avoided previous violations of Cambodian neutrality, Ford spoke in the House: "I can say without hesitation or qualification that I know of no Presidents . . . who have been false or deceptive in the information that has come from the White House."

But he did know. More careful House Republicans were sometimes outraged watching Ford mouthing little speeches delivered moments before by White House messengers from the offices of Nixon aides Charles Colson and Kenneth Clawson. "He didn't even bother to read the damn things," said a colleague. "If the White House wanted something said, Jerry just jumped up and said it."

Republican frustration with Ford, however, was a fleeting thing. As much as the word can be used between politicians, Ford was loved by the men and women he led in the House. His Republican colleagues tended to repeat themselves in discussing Ford's personal qualities and eight years of leadership—"straight . . . very fair . . . decent . . . openminded . . . understanding . . . no arm-twisting."

"He didn't keep us together with intellectual brilliance, persuasion or pressure," said Guy Vander Jagt of Michigan. "He kept us together with his personality. We did it for Jerry!" And Paul (Pete) McCloskey of California, one of the most independent of the Republicans, who was still receiving favors from Ford even though he was speaking out against Nixon and the war in Vietnam, added: "I can get tears in my eyes when I think about Jerry Ford. We love him."

28

It was not an easy job, marshaling a minority party whose membership ranged from McCloskey and Donald Riegle of Michigan on the left to John Schmitz of California and John Ashbrook of Ohio on the right. But after a very sloppy start, Ford performed adequately by the standards Congress sets for such things. His scorecard was not quite as good as Halleck's, but when the Republican Policy Committee took an official position on bills, Ford usually delivered 85 to 95 per cent of his party in futile opposition to Great Society legislation in the Johnson years of 1966 to 1968, and the same percentage in support of Nixon programs from 1969 to 1974. Robert L. Peabody, a Johns Hopkins University political scientist, evaluated Ford's performance during the Johnson years by interviewing seventy-five Republican House members; his conclusions included the following:

"A few Republicans thought Ford made a good over-all impression on the floor, despite his lack of debating skill and parliamentary adeptness . . . Others thought that Halleck, unlike Ford, drove some of his colleagues too hard. If anything, Ford appeared to err in the opposite direction.

"Certainly, his openness and sense of fairness were sources of strength. Members admired and appreciated these qualities. But other members deplored what they conceived to be a basic lack of political instinct and a hesitancy on Ford's part to utilize the full powers of his office. A comment from another party leader sums up the situation: 'Ford is very open-minded. Most of his problems come from the fact that he's too damned fair . . . You can't help but like and admire him. But when it comes to implementing a plan which requires a delicate sense of timing, a concern for the intricacies of details, an interweaving of the component parts, Ford is at a loss.' "

"He called us together on every important issue, no one had done that before," said Barber Conable, an upstate New York congressman who later moved into a leadership position under Ford. "He was very, very reluctant about deciding issues

29

himself. He encouraged divergent views . . . and he always wanted to be sure he hadn't forgotten anything. He liked to be well prepared."

Among Ford's problems in his first couple of years of leadership were Melvin Laird and the press. In some ways, Laird is everything Ford is not—one was apparently reading Machiavelli, while the other was memorizing football play-books—and one of the things Laird did as an "aide" to Ford in 1965 was to relieve the minority leader of the "burden" of hiring and directing minority staff. Ford went along with that, and Laird, with control of the staff, was well on the way to leading the minority leader. Goodell and Griffin invited Ford to lunch and another talk about the facts of political life.

With the press, Ford consistently fell into an old trap baited with the question, "What if that doesn't work, would you . . . ?" The minority leader would wake up with the next morning's New York *Times* and Washington *Post* to realize that reporters had led him into advocating the invasion of North Vietnam and into the middle of the flamboyant Democratic fight over seating Representative Adam Clayton Powell of Harlem. More lunches—Goodell and Griffin began to rehearse Ford at mock press conferences.

Not that Ford didn't want to invade North Vietnam. He probably did. But he didn't want to talk about it because by then Republican strategy was to blame the whole thing on Lyndon Johnson. Ford was a superhawk on Vietnam, and if that was essentially a conservative position, it was consistent with his congressional record.

As a congressman, Ford always made much of the fact that he was representing a conservative city—"Forget the voting record, that's Grand Rapids," he said after becoming Vice-President. But Grand Rapids, which elected a liberal Democrat to Congress as soon as Ford left, has almost certainly been more liberal than Gerald Ford for a good many years; his Grand Rapids, in fact, was a place and time crystallized

30

in memory. During his last ten years in the House, Ford's real constituency was the 140 to 191 Republican congressmen he led, and in the last five years his constituency was often one man, the man who led him, President Richard Nixon.

"The Nixon Presidency was to be something less than pure joy for House Minority Leader Ford," wrote Ford's old friend Jerald terHorst of the Detroit *News*. And that was an understatement. The new White House and Richard Nixon, Ford's friend of twenty-five years, played him like a yo-yo, sending him on improbable and unpleasant public errands, like flip-flopping for and against a contempt of Congress citation for CBS because the network refused to release research material on a controversial television documentary, "The Selling of the Pentagon." The reward for such blind loyalty was disdain; John Ehrlichman sat in his White House office one day in 1971, saying, "What a jerk Jerry is."

It was a confusing time for Ford, a man of very limited emotional range and discrimination—his enthusiastic assessment of almost anyone he meets is, "Gee, what a great guy!"— and bitterness is generally outside that range. The most he could do was occasionally say to a friend, "I wonder if the President knows what people are doing in his name."

Still, he did what he was told. He dropped his evangelical opposition to wage and price controls and "Red imperialism" as soon as Nixon changed directions and decided to impose controls and to visit the Reds in Peking and Moscow. And he did more than that to prove his devotion.

On September 25, 1973, Vice-President Spiro Agnew called on House Speaker Carl Albert to schedule "a full inquiry"—in effect, an impeachment—into reports that the United States attorney in Maryland was preparing to seek an Agnew indictment for bribery and income tax invasion while Agnew was a county executive, governor of Maryland and Vice-President. Agnew, of course, was trying to prevent court action and possibly jail by moving the investigation into the more comfortable climes of the House. And Ford, after conferring with the White House, was with him. When Albert rejected Agnew the next day, Ford called the decision "political . . . unfortunate."

What was really political and unfortunate was that Ford knew there was overwhelming evidence that Spiro Agnew was a crook and had taken envelopes filled with cash even as Vice-President. The minority leader had been informed of the evidence by Attorney General Elliot Richardson in a vain attempt to keep him from playing partisan politics with the Agnew matter or making a fool of himself. Agnew resigned fifteen days later, pleading "no contest" to income tax evasion charges and signing a forty-page statement of other charges—and sending Ford a note of "gratitude and affection."

Maybe the slowly dawning realization that Agnew and Ehrlichman and the others doing things in the President's name were not such great guys was beginning to take its toll on Ford. He sometimes promised his wife, Betty, that he would retire when his next term ended in January 1977. They had sat in the kitchen of their $75,000 split-level on Crownview Drive in Alexandria and calculated his pension rights against the costs of putting the children through college. Maybe it was time, he said, although Betty told friends she wasn't sure he would really do it.

Some friends thought Betty Ford was wrong, that her husband really did plan to quit—he had, in fact, begun consulting his businessmen buddies about becoming a "corporate representative," a lobbyist—but all that changed on October 10, when Agnew resigned. Within ten minutes of the news of the resignation, two Republican representatives, Jack Kemp of New York and Dan Kuykendall of Tennessee, were circulating petitions on the House floor urging Nixon to appoint Ford as Vice-President—and the minority leader happily watched them.

The ceremony to introduce Nixon's choice was set for the night of October 12, but the name of the Vice-President-

32

designate was still a secret that evening. Nixon loved his surprises. At 7:30, as the Fords were getting ready for dinner before going over to the White House for the announcement, President Nixon telephoned and said, "Jerry, Al Haig has a message for you." The White House chief of staff came on the line and said, "I've got good news for you. The President wants you to be Vice-President."

For months after that, Vice-President Ford began almost every speech with a charming family-at-home anecdote about how surprised all the Fords were that night. The other Fords may have been surprised, but Gerald Ford surely was not. He had gotten the word that morning from Melvin Laird, who was then a counselor to Nixon. In the afternoon, Barber Conable had told Ford on the House floor that he was going back to Rochester that night to make a speech instead of going to the scheduled presentation of the new Vice-President. "You might want to be there, Barb," Ford said.

"The only reason I'd go there is if it's you," said Conable, who thought the secrecy of the announcement and soliciting of sealed Vice-Presidential ballots from Congress was another Nixon charade. "I'll only go if you ask me."

"I'm asking you," Ford said.

"Can I draw any inference from that?" Conable said with a smile.

Ford smiled back. "I'm asking you."

2

The Vice-President

"I am a Ford, not a Lincoln . . . I am proud
—very proud—to be one of 200 million Americans. I promise my fellow citizens only this:
To uphold the Constitution, to do what is right
as God gives me to see the right, and within
the limited powers and duties of the Vice-
Presidency, to do the very best that I can for
America."

Gerald R. Ford,
December 6, 1973

ERALD FORD was not Richard Nixon's first choice. He was his last choice, in more ways than one. In the privacy of his own White House, Nixon had contempt for Ford—to the point, according to one man on the President's staff at the time, that he had Haig deliver the "good news" to Ford because he literally could not bring himself to do it.

The man Nixon wanted to appoint, insisted on appointing, was John Connally, the former Democratic governor of Texas who had become a Republican and his secretary of the Treasury. The President insisted while his advisers—particularly Alexander Haig, his chief of staff, and Melvin Laird, his most important counselor—argued vehemently that Connally would never be confirmed by Congress. The Texan was too controversial and too dangerous, he was a political turn-coat whose extensive business dealings at home and in Washington were too vulnerable to FBI checks and confirmation hearings under the 25th Amendment.

The Nixon Presidency was already in serious trouble because of investigations of "dirty tricks" in his 1972 campaign, and Haig and Laird repeatedly warned Nixon in the days after Agnew resigned that he could not afford a battle with Congress. Even Nelson Rockefeller and Ronald Reagan, the

governors of New York and California, would mean trouble—
they had too many enemies in both parties. It had to be Jerry
Ford, one of Congress's own.

"Nixon hated the idea, but he had to go along," said a White
House staffer. "There was also the other thing, that so many
people thought Ford was too dumb to be President. Impeachment really didn't seem possible then, but certainly no one
would think of doing it if it was going to put Jerry Ford in the
White House. It seemed perfect."

So it did. House Speaker Carl Albert lobbied for Ford.
Senator Strom Thurmond of South Carolina, the mean, sur-
viving soldier of the Old Confederacy, was "extremely
pleased." Senator Charles Percy of Illinois, a more liberal
Republican, praised the nominee as "an exceptional man."
Senator Walter Mondale of Minnesota, a liberal Democrat,
said: "The President is to be congratulated."

The Ford appointment was the first test of the 25th Amendment to the Constitution, adopted in 1967, providing that a
vacancy in the office of Vice-President would be filled by appointment of the President and confirmation by both houses
of Congress. The process proved to be historic in style and
journalistic in substance. Senators and representatives reacted
to the issues and stories of the day and proved conclusively
that Gerald R. Ford was not Spiro T. Agnew. The former
Vice-President had left office legally declining to contest Federal charges that he was a thief. The confirmation hearings
proved that the prospective Vice-President was not, concentrating on matters such as the Ford family's financing of a
condominium in Colorado ski country. He was earning about
$75,000 a year in salary and speech fees, paying his taxes,
buying a little property, and putting his children through
school—all of which was relief and refreshment to a country
whose Vice-President was on court-ordered probation and
whose President had bought two palmy estates in three years,
a guarded villa on the Atlantic for short weekends and a
guarded villa on the Pacific for long weekends.

The Senate approved the Ford nomination by a vote of

40

92 to 3 and the House by 387 to 35. On December 6, 1973, Gerald Ford was sworn in as the fortieth Vice-President of the United States.

Ford's qualifications for national leadership, which might have been examined in an election or at least questioned by opponents, were not a major public concern for his congressional fellows. The press, too, focused on his tax returns, although there were occasional printed reminders that Ford was quite accurate in pointing out that he was no Abraham Lincoln. "The Michigan congressman isn't a creative man," reported the *Wall Street Journal*. "Rather he is a pleasant but plodding party wheelhorse who often speaks and apparently thinks in clichés." *Newsweek* said: "This is Your Veep turned out to be Gerald Ford, the square-jawed, long-time House Republican leader, whose chief distinction in a quarter century in Washington has been unswerving loyalty to the GOP— and to Richard Nixon."

In *The New Yorker*, Richard Rovere sounded like Eustace Tilley peering through his monocle: "That he is thoroughly equipped to serve as Vice President seems unarguable; the office requires only a warm body and occasionally, a nimble tongue. However . . . neither Richard Nixon nor anyone else has come forward to explain Gerald Ford's qualifications to serve as Chief Executive. He altogether lacks administrative experience. If his knowledge of foreign affairs exceeds that of the average literate citizen, the fact has yet to be demonstrated . . . There is, of course, no Constitutional or other requirement that a potential President produce evidence of powers of independent or critical thought, but it has been a common assumption of the electorate that the President of the United States should be a leader rather than a follower, and close scrutiny of Gerald Ford's record over the past quarter century shows him to be a follower rather than a leader— except in the President's favorite sport, football, in which Ford shone as varsity center at the University of Michigan in the early thirties."

Nixon, too, was still mocking his new Vice-President, if the words of the men around Nelson Rockefeller are to be trusted. After the former New York governor had met with the President, his aides told a few reporters that Nixon had leaned back laughing and said: "Can you imagine Jerry Ford sitting in this chair?"

APRIL 20, 1974, was the last day of the week in which the new special prosecutor, Leon Jaworski, subpoenaed sixty-four White House tapes and memoranda, and the Labor Department announced that the Gross National Product was dropping at the sharpest rate since 1958 while inflation was rising at an annual rate of 14.5 per cent. Elizabeth Drew of *The New Yorker* visited the White House that day and recorded in her Watergate diary: "There is no way things can come out well, and there is a feeling of inevitability about what still has to be gone through. The President is finished anyway, and will be unable to govern."

Vice-President Ford, meanwhile, was in San Jose, California, sitting in the corner of a cavernous KNTV studio for a "Conversation with the Vice-President," to be televised that night on several California stations. At times, while the lights and cameras were being adjusted, the only sound in the huge, chilly room was the light snoring of Robert T. Hartmann, Ford's chief of staff and speech writer. It was usually that way in the afternoon after Hartmann had begun drinking.

The last question was asked by Bill Best of KNTV: How does it feel to be that close to the Presidency, closer really than a heartbeat away?

43

"The truth is I don't think about it," Ford answered.

The Vice-President was either a liar or a fool. The truth was that Ford was obsessed and confused. In long conversations with friends, he talked about being President, about wanting to be President, asserting that he could be a good President, then wondering how any President could succeed coming into office the way he would, through Nixon's disgrace.

When he became Vice-President, Ford called on Charles Goodell, as he called on many friends, and said: "Charlie, you and Bob Griffin got me into this, now you're going to have to help me out." Their advice, as summarized by one of them, was consistent: "You are the most powerful Vice-President in the history of the country. Nixon needs you more than you need him . . . Stay away from the White House, travel, get out of Washington . . . Don't get drawn into it. Don't listen to the tapes."

Ford tried to follow the advice. Although he was sometimes drawn back to Washington for long, rambling, almost incoherent conversations with Nixon, Ford flew more than 100,000 miles as Vice-President, making almost 500 public appearances in forty states, defending the President at every one: "He's been my friend for twenty-five years. He is my friend. I believe he is innocent of any charges." *

The traveling days were long and often disillusioning for the small band of men and women who went along. Usually there were a half-dozen staff members and a dozen reporters and photographers on Air Force Two, a slightly dented, pro-

* There was much reporting of "zigzagging" by Ford during his Vice-Presidency. But most of the zigzagging was by the press. Any change in the Vice-President's words or even inflection when mentioning Nixon and Watergate were instantaneously broadcast nationally as a new direction. One of his most celebrated zigs, for instance, a March 30 attack on "an arrogant, elite guard of political adolescents like CREEP" was within the context of support for regular Republican organizations and was followed by: "I'm not blaming the President for CREEP. He picked people he thought would do a good job. Unfortunately, they made mistakes."

44

peller-driven Convair, twenty years older than the small Grumman jet preferred by Agnew. Among themselves, the staff kindly described Ford's political style as "foible identification"—the average American could see himself in Ford's little blunders and mispronunciations. It was harder for reporters, who badly wanted the Vice-President to shine for the sake of the country and their own careers, and it was not an unusual event when a network television correspondent burst into a room full of other camp followers and shouted: "Jesus! He's the Vice-President of the United States. Doesn't he understand that?"

That was said just after the Vice-President of the United States had held a news conference in Troy, Michigan, and without being asked, brought up busing sixteen times in seventeen minutes—at a time when some local officials were saying the Detroit area was close to large-scale violence over busing disputes. That night on television, the people of Detroit saw and heard their Vice-President sounding like the Republican county chairman of a very small county, repeatedly implying that the Democratic party and any fellow travelers were essentially dedicated to dragging blue-eyed children into the blackest wilds.

How could he do that? Did he really want to be that divisive? I asked Ford a few days later. "It gets tough," he said, talking about shifting back and forth from national leader to Republican circuit rider. "But it's in the political pot already, and all I'm doing is giving the electorate the opportunity to understand there are differences between Republicans and Democrats."

"Look," he finally said, "what I was doing there was laying the groundwork for the campaign in my old district in November." Ford had been stunned when the Fifth District of Michigan had elected a Democrat to replace him after he resigned to become Vice-President—and as Vice-President, at least for those seventeen minutes, he couldn't rise above being a congressman from Grand Rapids.

Ford's travels took up almost half his time as Vice-President. It wasn't hard for him—he could take a helicopter from the center of Washington to Andrews Air Force Base, fifteen miles away in Maryland, and be off in minutes. He was getting as many as 900 invitations a week, mostly from county Republican organizations and old friends in Congress who needed help raising money back home.

"I'm getting out and seeing the people, listening to them," he said again and again. He did see a lot of people, but few who could not have been satirized by Sinclair Lewis. Gerald Ford's "people," Gerald Ford's America, was a mind-blurring parade of middle-aged men in double-knit suits—the small businessmen and corporate executives who are the core and soul of the Republican party—holding plastic cups of Scotch at $25-a-couple receptions in the Windsor Rooms of motels outside medium-sized cities. After one of those long nights, I asked him if he planned to see and hear non-Republican Americans, and he answered that he already had: "I'm going to have a private meeting tomorrow with another nonpartisan group, the directors of the Hearst Corporation."

None of that marked a change in career life style for Ford, who used to make 200 speeches a year on the road as House minority leader—successful politicians are the only men able to spend their time starring at pep rallies after they leave college. That life style, unfortunately, must turn their minds to oatmeal. One April day, the Vice-President spent an hour and a half at a head table next to Governor Ronald Reagan of California. Reporters asked later whether they had been talking about the 1976 Presidential election, and Ford answered: "No, we spent our time talking about the problems of 1974."

They had been in animated conversation, with great movement of arms and thoughtful pauses, and, it was true, they were not talking about 1976. I happened to hear everything they said because the microphone between them was open, and their words were piped into an empty back room. They spent the whole time talking about their weight problems and the relative merits of various diets and exercise machines.

46

On that same trip, Ford was trapped by a group of very serious businessmen at what was supposed to be a very casual get-together in a Palm Springs hotel. Suddenly he was fielding very real questions, and it was painfully obvious that he didn't have answers. The Vice-President of the United States —uninformed and inaccurate—stumbled and mispronounced his way through a long discussion of American policy in Cambodia, saying things like: "The situation in Cambodia is, uh, one of the most confused that we, or other nations, face in, uh, diplomacy or military circumstances. It's a very complex situation where you have, uh, the People's Republic of China, to a degree, anyhow, however, up until recently, apparently, supporting Prince Sihanouk. The implications are, uh, hard to detect, at the moment . . . In the meantime, it's a difficult situation, uh, but for us to leave with those other forces all confused, uh, would be a mistake, in my judgment."

Ford's days in the Capitol were few, and after his customary hour or so each morning reading the New York *Times* and Washington *Post,* he sat in, politely and quietly, at meetings in the White House, gave long interviews to almost anyone who asked—the first "exclusive" with *U. S. News and World Report* was headlined "Ford: Why I Will Not Run in '76" —and wrestled with a problem he would never solve, putting together a national-class staff.

Bob Hartmann was the king of Gerald Ford's hill—and it was a pretty low hill. Hartmann, a 56-year-old former Washington bureau chief of the Los Angeles *Times,* worked three years for Melvin Laird in the House before joining Ford in 1969, when Laird became secretary of Defense. By 1974, he was the Vice-President's speech writer and confidant, the first and last man to talk with Ford every day and on every issue. "Alter ego" is a term overused in politics, but it applied to Ford-Hartmann: Bob Hartmann seemed to be the dark side of sunny Jerry Ford.

Hartmann was nasty, vindictive and loud—and that was when he was sober. When he had been drinking, which seemed to be every day, he made an obvious effort to keep his voice

47

down. The lower tones sometimes made him more bearable; between the whispering and slurring it was often hard to tell whom he was insulting or picking on. He loved to pick on people who couldn't fight back.

I first saw Hartmann—or, rather, a flushed-faced little man I did not know who looked like an overweight welterweight —in the doorway at a Ford press conference in Chicago in March. The man was trying to hit a young Secret Service man who had asked, very politely, for his credentials. "Don't need goddamn . . ." the man huffed, swinging wild little punches into the air. Someone finally straightened the mess out, Hartmann straightened up and walked by the agent snarling, literally snarling, "You think you'll like it in Alaska? Huh? Huh?"

Reactions to Hartmann among other Ford people ranged from controlled dislike to hatred. Betty Ford tended toward the latter, letting reporters know that she appreciated any efforts that might reduce his influence on her husband. But while you might not want your daughter to marry him, Hartmann was very competent at what he did—write Ford's speeches and give him unvarnished political truth. For your own sake, Hartmann nagged, get out of town until the Watergate investigations run their course. American politics and politicians being what they were, the advice had merit, as Hartmann's advice usually did. It is a comment on Gerald Ford and his profession that the most talented man around him as congressman, Vice-President and President was an abusive pragmatist whose sole consideration was the politics of the moment.

With Hartmann on top, the rest of the staff had an air of timidity about it, but they were nice people, reflections of the Vice-President's bluff, Midwestern good humor. Unfortunately, they were also in over their heads and had a habit of forgetting things—appointments in Washington, baggage in Denver. Paul Miltich, Ford's press secretary and a former Washington correspondent for a string of Michigan newspapers, would forget to tell reporters that while the Vice-President was playing golf in Monterey, California, he took time off between the fifth and sixth holes to make a telephone address to the Maine State Republican Convention. When their home offices inevitably called the reporters with Ford to ask about his Maine remarks, the reporters told their bosses not to be ridiculous, the Vice-President was putting out on the eighteenth hole.

On Air Force Two a couple of nights later, reporters were debating whether to complain to Ford about Miltich. They had just decided not to—Miltich was a nice guy and why get him in trouble—when Ford invited them back to share a birthday cake someone had given him in Palm Springs. Between bites and little jokes, Ford asked if anyone had ever been up in a hot air balloon. "It's terrific, a lot of fun," he said. He had been up in one yesterday with his son. "We got lost and everything. What a ride!" There was a greenish look on the faces of the reporters, and it had nothing to do with the cake; Miltich kind of backed out of the cabin. The Vice-President of the United States had been floating lost over Death Valley or someplace, and no one had known anything about it! The television correspondents had visions of being exiled to covering traffic jams in suburban Virginia if their bosses ever found out.

It was fun in those days. Ford was living like a super-congressman who did not even have to show up for roll call votes. The press was along for the ride. One morning, Ford was teeing off at Pebble Beach, California, and a dozen national reporters were standing around watching—notebook reporters were scribbling a little color, television reporters were shooting a little film. After Secret Service agents ran down the sunny fairway to protect the Vice-President and mark his golf balls, Ford belted out a drive and the reporters drove into Carmel for some shopping. They picked up an "Official U. S. Taxpayer" badge and an "Impeach President Ford" bumper sticker to give the Vice-President later.

"Is this what you people do all the time?" asked an incredulous young reporter from KCBS in Los Angeles.

Well, a lot of the time. Meanwhile, back in Washington it was raining and the country seemed to be falling apart.

ON APRIL 30, 1974, President Nixon released volumes of transcripts of taped White House conversations—incomplete, edited, but devastating—and "expletive deleted" became part of the American idiom. With the city of Washington stripped of its illusions—even Senate Minority Leader Hugh Scott, a reflexive Nixon defender, called the transcripts "shabby, disgusting, immoral"—the President traveled to the state of Washington to officially open a World's Fair in Seattle and referred to Governor Daniel Evans as "Governor Evidence."

Vice-President Ford said that he was "a little disappointed" when he read the transcripts. He also said that he was "convinced beyond any doubt that the President is innocent." Maybe he meant it, maybe he even read the transcripts. But he was already being told about the shape Nixon was in—the President was drinking and pounding his desk in the Oval Office, shouting, "I won't be bullied! I won't be bullied!"—and he was hearing more of Hartmann's hard-headed advice: do nothing that will make it appear that you are trying to take the Presidency from Nixon.

A few days later, Philip W. Buchen, one of the Vice-President's oldest friends and his first law partner back in

51

Grand Rapids, stopped by for dinner at the small George-town house of Clay T. Whitehead, the 35-year-old director of the White House Office of Telecommunications Policy. Buchen, who was something of a stranger in Washington, coming at Ford's request to head a Presidential commission on the rights of privacy, surprised Tom and Margaret White-head by saying, "We have to do some planning for Jerry. We have to face the fact that the President may resign."

The Grand Rapids lawyer said he had already discussed contingency planning with the Vice-President and that Ford had told him not to do it, that even talking about it would be disloyal. Still, Buchen told Whitehead it had to be done, and the young White House aide finally and reluctantly agreed —partly because, like others in the White House, he was worried about Nixon's mental condition.

Whitehead, who had served a minor role on the staff of the committee that coordinated the transition of the Presidency from Lyndon Johnson to Richard Nixon in 1969, called in three friends, three young men he trusted: Jonathan Moore, a former assistant to Attorney General Richardson, Lawrence Lynn, a Democrat and an assistant secretary of the Interior, and Brian Lamb, Whitehead's OTP assistant and a Democrat. As the Watergate scandals and the Nixon administration both unraveled, the four young men and Buchen met secretly for two months, poring over books about the transitions of power from Franklin D. Roosevelt to Harry S. Truman in 1945, and drew up a detailed schedule for the first days of the first unelected American President.

The worst Ford has ever been accused of on Watergate and the ensuing cover-up is devoted, perhaps calculated, blindness. He saw no evil. Although he met regularly with some of the men convicted later as Watergate conspirators, he was never near their tight inner circle, and no evidence has been presented that he ever participated in anything but casual Watergate conversations. Ford's own words about Watergate and the cover-up, however, have occasionally been

52

intriguing. While testifying at his confirmation hearings on November 16, 1973, before the House Judiciary Committee, the minority leader had this exchange with Representative George Danielson, a California Democrat:

DANIELSON: Have you at any time since June 17, 1972, the day of Watergate, spoken personally or by telephone with the President, Mr. Mitchell, the former attorney general, Mr. Haldeman, Mr. Ehrlichman, John Dean, Mr. Colson, Mr. Magruder, or anyone else at the White House concerning the raising of funds for the support of the families of the Watergate defendants?

FORD: None whatsover. Where I may have called, I might have casually said, in a meeting where there were a number of people that I thought it was, if it was being done, it ought to be stopped and if it was thought of as an undertaking, it ought not to be done.

That answer was quite different from Ford's usual replies to Watergate questions. Almost invariably, he answered with the three words "I did not." His words in this case would make it conceivable that the minority leader had been present, perhaps innocently, when someone mentioned support payments or "hush money" for the original Watergate burglars —certainly he was talking about Watergate with John Mitchell in the same period that Mitchell and others were talking about a cover-up.

On the record, Ford's first involvement with Watergate machinations came sometime after a September 15, 1972, Oval Office meeting between the President, his chief of staff, H. R. Haldeman, and counsel, John Dean. The subject of the meeting, according to the taped record, was the blocking of a proposed Watergate investigation by the House Banking and Currency Committee, chaired by Representative Wright Patman, a Texas Democrat. Nixon wanted his aides to get Ford to "work something out . . . This is a big play. He has to know it comes from the top."

Ford did hold two meetings with the fifteen Republicans

53

on the thirty-five-member committee, and the minority members later joined with five Democrats to block the Patman inquiry. "Another sigh of relief was made at the White House," Dean later testified, "we had leaped one more hurdle in the continuing cover-up."

Did that make Ford part of the cover-up? An unwitting part, perhaps. The minority leader insisted that he was not acting on White House orders when he convened the Republicans, but Ford had been doing exactly what the White House wanted him to do for four years; that did not mean, however, that he always knew why Nixon wanted it done. For Minority Leader Gerald Ford, the unashamed partisan, it was probably reason enough that any investigation before the 1972 elections might hurt his friend and party. His public record on Watergate over the next two years was touching, a monument to loyalty or stupidity.

On January 15, 1974, Ford traveled to Atlantic City, New Jersey, to address the American Farm Bureau Federation and recited a White House-written speech charging that impeachment talk was "a massive propaganda campaign" by such organizations as Americans for Democratic Action and organized labor to "dominate the Congress and, through it, the nation." In February, he was in Iowa, saying: "Let me say a word about a great American—the President of the United States . . . a man of integrity, ability and dedication and great intelligence . . . Mr. Nixon has done more for America than any President in our lifetime . . . I think he is as good if not better than any President in the history of our country." In March, he accused the House Judiciary Committee, which was hearing impeachment evidence, of being "out of control."

And so it went, with Ford punctuating his knee-jerk defense with statements like: "I will remain my own man, fly my own course, and speak my own convictions." In early April, he told the President he planned to fly his own course to Palm Springs, California, for a week of golf. As usual, the Fords planned to rent a condominium with a friend, Leon Parma, a California businessman. No, no, said the President, stay where I stay in Palm Springs, at Walter Annenberg's place.

Walter Annenberg was then the U. S. ambassador to Great Britain in addition to being the publisher of the Philadelphia *Inquirer* and *TV Guide* and a six-figure contributor to Nixon campaigns. His "place" was Sunnylands, a desert oasis half the size of Hoboken, New Jersey, with ten lakes, a twenty-seven-hole golf course, and ten-foot-high hedges and guard stations to keep the world out.

Didn't Ford think that kind of hibiscus isolation was one of the things the nation resented about Nixon? I asked him the day he left Sunnylands. "I don't understand why you say it's impolitic," Ford answered. "The President set it up with Annenberg when he heard Betty and I were going to Palm Springs. It was very pleasant . . . We loved it."

They hated it. The Annenberg servants ordered the Fords not to touch *objets d'art,* warned them not to take photographs inside the house, objected to their children's life style (which included one son's live-in girl friend), and refused to let Secret Service agents come inside for a glass of water in the ninety-degree desert sun.

Loyalty never seemed to ask too much of Gerald Ford. But by midsummer, the days were dwindling down for his patron. On July 25, in Washington, the members of the Judiciary Committee were on national television, each explaining why he or she would or would not vote the next day to recommend impeachment of the President to the full House of Representatives. In Muncie, Indiana, Ford emotionally and dramatically told a crowd, "I can say from the bottom of my heart that the President of the United States is innocent . . . He is right!"

The next day, the Judiciary Committee voted 27 to 11 to send to the House the first article of impeachment, which began: "In his conduct of the office of President of the United States, Richard M. Nixon, in violation of his Constitutional oath . . ."

After condemning the Judiciary vote as "partisan," the

Vice-President resumed his travels and his defense, telling crowds in California and Nevada that he did not believe there was evidence of impeachable offenses by Nixon. Returning to Washington late on July 31, he received a call from General Alexander Haig, who had replaced Haldeman as the President's chief of staff. Haig used the word "urgent" and the two men met early the next morning, August 1, in Ford's office in the Executive Office Building. Haig told the Vice-President that new tape evidence would be surrendered to Judge John Sirica within four days, on Monday, August 5, and that the new evidence would probably lead to the impeachment of Nixon by the House and trial in the Senate.

The Vice-President met with Hartmann and Buchen through most of the morning and then received another call from Haig. The two men sat down again at 3:30 P.M. in the same office.

"Are you ready to take over the Presidency?" were the Haig words that Ford remembered later. "The substance of his conversation," Ford said, "was that the new disclosure would be devastating, even catastrophic, insofar as President Nixon was concerned."

Ford and Haig talked for forty-five minutes. Haig brought up the possibility of a Ford pardon for Nixon if the President resigned—it was one of several options Haig said were being discussed at the White House, including a self-pardon by Nixon—but Ford later testified that he did not commit himself on a pardon or anything else. In fact, Ford said, he refused to offer any advice to Nixon, he just listened. He called Haig late the next afternoon to make or repeat the point that he wanted no part in the President's consideration of whether or not to resign.*

* Ford's version of the conversations with Haig during the first week in August was contained in testimony he gave before a subcommittee of the House Judiciary Committee on October 17. Possibly the first President to testify before a congressional inquiry, he said he wanted to assure the American people there was "no deal" involved in his eventual pardon of Nixon for possible Watergate crimes.

56

Ford left the White House chief of staff to meet his wife and inspect the new Vice-Presidential residence on the Naval Observatory grounds, the house they were supposed to move into. "I went through this routine for an hour," he said later. "She had all these plans where this piece of furniture was going here and that was going there. Then I went back to the office. Then I went home, and while we were changing clothes I said, 'Betty, the probability of us living in that house is very remote.' And I told her what had happened."

And what would Ford tell the country? He would lie and say he still believed Nixon was innocent. The Vice-President took off again, this time for Mississippi and Louisiana, where he said, on August 4, "I believe the President is innocent. I don't want any impression created that I've changed my mind about the President's innocence."

The next day, August 5, the White House released the June 23, 1972, transcript of a tape made in the Oval Office six days after the Watergate break-in, the tape in which the President of the United States ordered his men to try to block the Federal Bureau of Investigation from investigating the burglary.

On Tuesday night, August 6, Alexander Haig telephoned the Vice-President and told him to expect to be President within seventy-two hours. Ford called Buchen, and his old friend formally told him of the existence of the transition planning group that had been meeting in Whitehead's home. And it was a formality—Ford had been aware of the transition planning for at least two weeks. But he had never been directly told, so that he could maintain the public fiction that he had no knowledge of it. In politics, the man out front prefers to have a clear conscience when he denies the truth. Ford, however, did not let conscience get in his way the next day when he told the New York *Times* that there had been no planning for a Presidential transition.

Buchen asked the Vice-President who else he wanted involved in the final planning. Ford gave him five names:

Senator Griffin, former Pennsylvania Governor William W. Scranton, who had served in the House with Ford; former Wisconsin congressman John Byrnes; Bryce Harlow, a former Eisenhower and Nixon aide now working as a lobbyist for Proctor & Gamble; and William S. Whyte, a close friend and chief lobbyist of U. S. Steel.

"What about Mel Laird?" Buchen asked.

No. Ford did not really trust Laird, even though he regularly sought his advice. Mel Laird, who had almost taken Ford over in the House ten years ago, was already giving the impression that he would be the real power behind a President Ford. Laird had a way of being in on crucial, secret things that somehow weren't secret any more when morning newspapers had stories of his key behind-the-scenes role.

The expanded transition group met in Whyte's home, putting together a fifty-page loose-leaf binder laying out the first days and weeks of a Ford administration—it looked very much like a football play-book. There was one bad moment while they worked Wednesday night, August 7. Griffin received a phone call from Nixon's son-in-law, Edward Cox, who said the President had just met with his family and was in "an extremely bad emotional state." Cox said he thought there was a chance Nixon might not resign after all.

But he did, of course. Within thirty-six hours, Gerald Ford would be the thirty-eighth President of the United States. It was a job his son Michael, a 23-year-old divinity student, had not wished for his father: "Dad might be thrown into the lions' pit and have everything he has built up torn apart."

3

The New President

"I stood on my balcony and watched that chopper taking Nixon away after he resigned, and it was like I was coming out of Buchenwald. In that mood, even a 35-cent hamburger tastes like steak."

Mel Elfin,
Washington Bureau Chief of *Newsweek*

AMERICA loved President Ford. The past, his and Richard Nixon's and everybody's, was forgotten for a euphoric moment of history. Nixon, facing certain impeachment and conviction, dictated a single sentence, signed his name under it and a messenger handed it to Secretary of State Henry Kissinger at 11:35 A.M., August 9, 1975: "I hereby resign as President of the United States."

Kissinger was the first secretary of State ever to act out the Constitutional script for a Presidential resignation. At 12:05, Gerald R. Ford put his hand on a family Bible open to Proverbs, Chapter 3, verses 5 and 6:

> Trust in the Lord with all thine heart;
> And lean not unto thine own understanding.
> In all thy ways acknowledge him,
> And he shall direct thy paths.

He was the President of the United States. The internal loudspeaker system in the White House cleared its electronic throat and said, "The President will meet with his senior staff in the Roosevelt Room . . ." There was something extraordinary about that message—only minutes before the same distant voices had said "The President . . ." and had meant not Gerald Ford, but Richard Nixon. Two dozen people began walking toward the room named for the Republican Roosevelt, Theodore. Ford walked in and they stood, some self-consciously, and the President said he wanted no *pro forma* resignations of Nixon people—they were all to stay on, for now. General Alexander Haig, Nixon's chief of staff and now Ford's, rose and pledged the loyalty of the group "in our hour of common cause."

But moments later, there was a break in the common cause of the old Nixon people and the Ford transition team. The Ford people waited to escort the new President to the White House press room in the West Wing. "There's no time for that," snapped Haig, a crisp man, and a phalanx of the chief of staff's assistants swept Ford past his confused men. "We literally had to sneak a note past Haig's men to get the President out," said Tom Whitehead, who was acting as secretary to the Ford transition team.

Over Haig's protest, the new President walked the few steps to the press briefing lobby, a room built over the swimming pool where Franklin D. Roosevelt had exercised and Lyndon B. Johnson occasionally skinny-dipped with friends late at night. The President said he considered the reporters "friends" —and many were—and said his press secretary would be one of them, Jerald F. terHorst of the Detroit *News*. "Could you hold Jerry up for us to see, Mr. President?" yelled Peter Lisagor of the Chicago *Daily News*—terHorst is a short man. The President laughed; everyone laughed—there was a new President. Richard Nixon was gone.

After Ford left for a series of cameo meetings with foreign ambassadors, terHorst, a friend of the President's for twenty-five years, took the questions of his former colleagues in the unique daily ritual known as the White House briefing. The last question referred to Ford's comments on a possible pardon for President Nixon during the minority leader's Vice-Presidential confirmation hearings: "I do not think the public would stand for it," Ford had said on November 16, 1973.

"Can you check for us," a reporter asked, "as to if President Ford's position is still as he stated on the Hill, that he is not in favor of immunity?"

"Yes," terHorst answered, "I can assure you of that."

"He is not in favor of immunity?"

"I can assure you of that."

At 5:30 P.M., after small talk and earnest photographs with fifty-eight ambassadors, Ford went into the Cabinet room to talk about being President of the United States. There were nine other men in the room as the President entered. They all stood. On one side of the table was the official transition team, four men personally selected by Ford. All four had served with him in Congress—Secretary of the Interior Rogers C. B. Morton, NATO Ambassador Donald Rumsfeld, William Scranton and John O. Marsh, an extremely conservative Democrat from Virginia. With them were Haig, Phil Buchen, Bob Hartmann, William Seidman, a millionaire accountant from Grand Rapids, and Whitehead, the principal author of the unofficial transition schedule. The occasion seemed historic to some—they took notes and their recollections of the meeting were vivid.

"Sit down, sit down," Ford said. "Well, here we are . . . There's one person sitting here who's going to have a big role in this administration and doesn't know it."

"John," he said, turning to his old friend Marsh on his left, "you're going to be my counselor for National Security and International Affairs."

Marsh mumbled "Thank you, Mr. President," but he paled. He had, in effect, been given a job that was already filled— by Henry Kissinger. He remained silent as Ford kept talking, then listened to a check list of items and options from the transition schedule. After most of them, Ford turned to Haig and said, "Al, what do you think of that?"

Haig was a commanding presence, making one concise recommendation after another, then ending with "if you think it's best, Mr. President." Each time Ford would nod, "Yes, okay."

65

The Ford team tried to shift control by asking Ford how he wanted to organize the White House.

"Well," the President said, "I like to start work at about eight o'clock and do routine work at first. I like to start meeting people at about ten . . . I don't like long memos, I listen better than I read, really . . . I like to take reading home, but not a great volume . . . I also like yes/no options without a lot of complications."

Finally the President stood up and said he had to leave. Everyone else stood and as Ford started to walk out, Marsh called, "Mr. President! Mr. President, sir. I appreciate the honor you've just given me, but I don't think I should do it . . . Sir, won't it raise questions about Henry Kissinger's authority?"

"Oh, my God," Ford said. "I never thought about that. Maybe I shouldn't—what do you think, Al?"

Haig said that Marsh could be made a counselor without specific title, "if you think that's best, Mr. President."

"Good idea," the President said, "let's do that."

If the new President sounded a bit shaky, only ten men knew. The rest of the nation did not know and did not want to know. For the moment it was enough that Jerry Ford was a nice guy. There was thrilling false dawn, the era of good feeling, English muffins, early morning swims. *Time* magazine reported "a mood of good feeling and even exhilaration in Washington that the city had not experienced for many years." And "a senior Nixon staff official" was quoted in the Washington *Post* as offering the opinion that "this is the first truly normal President we've had since George Washington."

"I expect to follow my instincts of openness and candor," Ford had said immediately after his swearing-in on August 9. What he was particularly open to was photographs. On the first Sunday of his Presidency, Ford invited five photographers to watch and click as he swam sixteen forty-foot laps in his backyard pool in Alexandria. "This isn't burlesque," he cracked as the cameraman recorded the slipping off of his maroon bathrobe—and it wasn't, but it was terrific public relations. The new President hardly went anywhere or did anything without the shuttering presence of his personal photographer, David Kennerly, a 27-year-old Pultizer Prize winner from *Time*—Kennerly replaced the Polaroid camera in the corner of Ford's old congressional office—and others permanently recording "intimate" First Family moments. Politicians, actors and reporters are probably the only human beings who consider life intimate when a stranger with a camera is in the room.

That afternoon, Sunday, Ford went back to the Oval Office and met separately with a dozen old friends from Congress, discussing the next Vice-President. He asked for their advice in the Ford manner, lining up other men's opinions and feelings, checking to make sure he had not overlooked anything important, ready to accommodate himself. "What kind of Vice-President do you want to have?" asked Barber Conable of New York. "Wait a minute," Ford said, "I want you to tell me what kind I should have."

Like many public men, Conable keeps a dictated journal, and one of his entries after that conversation was intriguing: "He asked me to help him. He told me I knew him better than he knew himself."

Who am I? How did I get *here?* Well, first Jerry Ford was a nice guy—Conable felt embarrassed because he called him "Jerry" three times instead of "Mr. President"—and that was what came across first. Some of Ford's folksiness was calculated, but much of it was real. When he was still Vice-President, he was not above lifting a few with the crew that traveled in his wake. More than that, he did not always choose his companions by rank.

Flying from Monterey to Palm Springs, California, late one night, Vice-President Ford wandered up to the press section of Air Force Two—his predecessor, Spiro Agnew, usually barred the press from his plane—and spent an hour schmoozing and boozing with three television technicians. They talked about hunting, mortgages and his days as a forest ranger years ago in Yellowstone National Park.

That is not the way it is usually done. Most major politicians cannot tell the difference between cameramen and cameras. When politicians do their airplane visiting, they usually seek out reporters with clout, network correspondents or reporters from *Time* or the New York *Times.*

That night, in fact, Patrick Anderson, on assignment for the New York *Times Magazine,* was sitting behind Ford and the technicians. The plane dropped into a tremendous air pocket and Anderson's drink, a Scotch and water, arced gracefully onto the bald head of the Vice-President of the United States, then dribbled over his ears and onto the shoulders of his new double-knit. Anderson started to mumble mortified apologies, but Ford cut him off with "Aw, forget it" and his high horsey laugh.

"What a guy," Anderson said. "If he was a little more liberal, I'd go to work for him."

That side of Jerry Ford—he really is an unpretentious, unassuming man—came across, and across, and across in the innocent days of August 1974. Harlem's Congressman Charles Rangel, no fan of Ford or his civil rights voting record, received a telephone call on August 12; his secretary said, winking: "There's a call from somebody saying he's the President." It was the President. "Hi, Charlie," he said and invited the Congressional Black Caucus to come to the White House. Two days later, when an invited group of mayors was there, the President slipped into the East Room unnoticed and began walking up to the ones he had never met, sticking out his hand and saying, "Hi, I'm Jerry Ford."

Jerry Ford touched all the bases. He worked the delegation of mayors and the country like the crowd at a Republican fund-raiser. He invited George Meany, the cantankerous president of the AFL-CIO, in for a forty-five-minute chat; he invited in 300 middle-level Federal appointees, asked for their help, then shook 300 hands while a camera clicked 300 times; he proclaimed "Women's Equality Day" with his wife at his side; posed with "The Farm Family of The Year," the Fowlers of Fairbanks, Alaska; called in leaders of senior citizens' organizations; and in an inspired little drama personally announced and presented a promotion to Air Force General Daniel (Chappie) James, who was both the highest-ranking black man in the armed forces and the officer in charge of Prisoner of War and Missing in Action programs of the Vietnam war.

On the eleventh day of his Presidency, August 19, Ford left Washington for the first time to speak to the national convention of the Veterans of Foreign Wars in Chicago. It was another good day—citing Abraham Lincoln and Harry S Truman, he called for conditional amnesty for Vietnam "offenses loosely described as desertion and draft-dodging."

The VFW speech was the most striking example to date that Richard Nixon was gone, showing a President compassionately aware of the divisions among Americans: "I want them to come home if they want to work their way back . . . these young Americans should have a second chance to contribute their fair share to the rebuilding of peace among ourselves and with all nations. So I am throwing the weight of the Presidency on the side of leniency."

A week later in Columbus, Ohio, for an address at Ohio State University, Ford was grabbed by a woman who said, "Where's Betty?"

"She's working," Ford said.

"You guys are going to bring back marriage again!"

Gerald Ford certainly seemed to be bringing something back, even if it was just ladies in Columbus happily shouting at their President. The New York *Times* commissioned a national Gallup poll which showed that 71 per cent of Americans approved of their new President's performance, while only 3 per cent had unfavorable impressions. Hugh Sidey of *Time* magazine, the semiofficial chronicler of the good that Presidents do, declared to ten million readers: "Everywhere there was the feeling that the American Presidency was back in the possession of the people."

WHILE President Ford happily posed for happy photographers, Alexander Haig and Henry Kissinger ran the country.

Symbolically, the transition plan begun in Tom Whitehead's home was clicking toward perfection. The transition schedule, refined in the last hours of the Nixon Presidency by a group personally approved by Ford, listed three priority goals for the new administration:

"1. Restoration of the confidence and trust of the American people in their political leadership, institutions and processes. This is the major principle and others relate to it.

2. Assumption of control which is firm and efficient.

3. National feeling of unification and reconciliation enabled by the character and style of the new President." *

* The priority goals were on the first page of the fifty-page looseleaf binder given to Ford by Buchen on the night he took the oath as President. The transition book included an almost hour-by-hour public schedule for the first two weeks of the new administration, and Ford followed it almost exactly. The makeup of the official transition team was also recommended, but Ford accepted only three of four recommendations—Morton as liaison to the Cabinet, Marsh as liaison to Congress, and Scranton as chief recruiter of new personnel. The fourth recommendation was Frank Carlucci, undersecretary of Health, Edu-

71

The meetings with Cabinet, staff and press, the touching bases and photographs with foreign power, labor, management, the elderly and the young, were telling the nation that the White House was open again. Confidence, trust, unification and reconciliation seemed more than just memo words.

"Everyone was so relieved and so drained and physically tired that it took a couple of days or so to realize something was missing, something was wrong," Whitehead said. "Then it became clearer and clearer what was missing: Jerry Ford, in his own mind, was not ready to be President of the United States."

Ford was not assuming control. The check list under the second priority of the transition schedule called for meetings of the major elements of the executive branch—the Cabinet, the White House staff, the Joint Chiefs of Staff and others for a single overriding purpose—to immediately assert the authority of President Gerald R. Ford. Included on the check list was the National Security Council, the preserve of Secretary of State Kissinger. But when Ford asked Kissinger to assemble the NSC on the second day of his Presidency, August 10, Kissinger said no. No, the secretary said, there was no reason to call the Council together, it would set a bad precedent to assemble the country's crisis-management group of civilian and military officials together unless there actually was a potential military crisis. Ford agreed—until Scranton later convinced him that he had to order Kissinger to assemble the council.

Kissinger and Ford spent hours alone together those first days in long briefing sessions, with Kissinger alternately regaling the new President with tales of his travels and emphasizing the dangers of any changes or new directions in American foreign policy. "Henry kept warning Ford that other nations

---

cation and Welfare, as liaison to the White House staff. Ford crossed out Carlucci's name and wrote in "Rumsfeld." As President, Ford nominated Carlucci as U.S. ambassador to Portugal.

would think that this was the time to take advantage of the United States," said a senior official. "There wasn't much he could do but let Henry run the show. There was never any question of moving Ford people into foreign policy. What could we do? Henry *was* American foreign policy."

On the domestic side, it was Haig, the former Army colonel, and then general, who came to national prominence as a Kissinger deputy on the National Security Council. "We had to keep Haig, he had all the clout in the government," said Jerry terHorst, Ford's first appointee and one of the few Ford men who actually had a desk in the White House in the first two weeks. "There was business in the pipelines of the government. We had to keep it moving, but we didn't even know where the pipelines were. And Haig made it clear that he had been running the government for the last eight or ten months of the Nixon Presidency."

One of the first priorities of the transition group—referred to in memos to Ford as "the interim staff"—was to establish a genuine Ford White House staff, not a Nixon staff operating under Ford. The transition loose-leaf book recommended that the new President "short-term" all Nixon staff, first getting rid of Press Secretary Ronald Ziegler and Roy Ash, director of the Office of Management and Budget, as prime symbols of the Nixon years.

"You must walk a delicate line between compassion and consideration for the former President's staff and the rapid assertion of your personal control over the executive branch," said one of the first memos to President Ford from his transition team. "The exception we recommend is Al Haig. Al has done yeoman service for his country. However, he should not be given the option to become *your* chief of staff."

The transition report also recommended dismissing the entire Cabinet except for Kissinger—Ford had already pledged to retain the secretary of State—and included a procedure for physically clearing all White House offices within seventy-two hours. None of that ever happened because Ford never decided whether or not to exercise that option; in effect, he decided not to.

It was immediately clear that Ford was personally reluctant to move quickly to change the Nixon White House, and it was decided at the transition team meeting the first day that Scranton should brief the President on the functions and operations of the White House staff. Haig volunteered to help and told Scranton he would schedule a meeting with the President at 9:30 the next morning, August 10. In fact, the August 10 schedule produced later by Haig's staff showed a meeting between Ford and Haig at 8:30 A.M.

When Scranton arrived at 9:30, he was met by Terry O'Donnel, who had been Nixon's appointments secretary; he was told that Ford and Haig were in conference, and his orders from Haig were not to disturb them. When the chief of staff came out of the Oval Office, he told Scranton the briefing was over, he had already handled it.

Within twenty-four hours there was an open struggle for power and control in the White House—"Byzantine" was the word terHorst used at home. There was even an informal investigation by some Ford people who were convinced old Nixon hands were smuggling cartons of damaging files out of the White House at night—personnel records with political references and evaluations, among them. But what could they prove? The Ford people did not know what records and legal documents were *in* the building—and the Nixon people weren't telling—so they could not very easily discover if any were being taken out.

The President, from the first day, was caught in the middle, or on top. He was spending a good part of his time listening to the complaints of the leaders of two separate and hostile staffs, Al Haig of the old and Bob Hartmann of the new.

"Haig would be in there saying, 'These people don't understand government, don't understand the risks,' " terHorst remembered. "Then it would be Hartmann saying, 'You want to know why it's screwed up? Because they're doing it all behind our backs, that's why. We have to get rid of . . .' " Hartmann

74

refused to attend the daily senior staff members' meetings presided over by Haig. When another Ford man asked him why, Hartmann was blunt as usual: "Fuck Haig. I work for the President."

"Ford knew what was going on," terHorst said, "but he didn't want to fire anybody. He didn't want to throw anyone out on the street." And the Nixon people just stayed. At press briefings, terHorst would announce that the Reverend John McLaughlin, a Jesuit priest who was paid $34,000 a year to do some speech-writing and a little controversial speechmaking for Nixon, was leaving the White House staff. Then Father McLaughlin would announce that he had no intention of leaving; he sat in the White House preparing a schedule for a speaking tour he said would convince the country to accept Ford as President.

"I've been criticized," Ford said later, "and I think this is somewhat legitimate, that I don't like to hurt people's feelings. And I can't say that I dislike anybody in the Nixon administration, so I've been very careful to move where I thought it was wise for a number of reasons. And it's the hardest thing for me to tell somebody that they ought to leave. And that's my nature, and I guess you're not going to change it. I haven't in sixty-one years."

The whole truth of the matter, however, was that the problem of really changing the Nixon staff and system went deeper than Ford's "nice guy" nature. "He was incapable of conceiving a different organization than what he had found; things like that were beyond him," said one of the new President's senior administrators. "As long as Haig was there with a system in place, Ford would be dependent—that's one of the reasons so many people wanted to get rid of Haig."

Even Haig wanted to get rid of McLaughlin, but he gave endless reasons why every other Nixon holdover was indispensable. Haig was pushed back only one step in the early days, when he struggled bitterly with terHorst after the press secretary accused White House counsel J. Fred Buzhardt of deliberately misleading him in an attempt to get the damning

Nixon tapes out of the White House and into the possession of the former President.

On August 14, terHorst announced that the tapes "have been ruled to be the personal property of former President Nixon." The ruling, he said, had been made by the White House legal staff with the agreement of the Justice Department and Special Watergate Prosecutor Leon Jaworski. "The decision was made independent of President Ford," terHorst added. "He concurs in the decision."

Buzhardt had informed terHorst of the ruling earlier in the day. The press secretary, concerned that there were still no Ford people on the legal staff, asked whether the Justice Department and special prosecutor were involved with the ruling. "They're aboard," was the answer, according to terHorst.

But within minutes of terHorst's announcement, when the news was broadcast, both Attorney General William Saxbe and Jaworski said they were never part of an agreement; Buzhardt had merely informed them of his own ruling. TerHorst, who had first told Ford of the agreement, went back to the President, embarrassed and angry—they had been taken. Buzhardt's resignation was announced the next day, August 15. (But only announced—Buzhardt, staying out of sight and mind of reporters, continued working at the White House until mid-October and was on the payroll almost to the end of the year. He only left when the Washington *Star* revealed his quiet tenure.)

Whether or not he had been conned, Ford did not overrule the tape decision for another day, acting on August 16, after outraged reaction from the Justice Department, courts and the press—and then the President only said he was "deferring" movement of the tapes.

There was also rage inside the White House, open arguments between Nixon people and Ford people over the pseudo-removal of "poor Fred," as the Nixon holdovers called him. Haig confronted terHorst and called him "the little executioner."

"Do you feel good, executing a sick man?" Haig asked, referring to the heart attack Buzhardt had had a few months before.

Ironically, and accidentally, Haig had been in the press briefing room when terHorst announced Buzhardt's "resignation." The chief of staff was taking Bob Hartmann and John Marsh on a tour of the West Wing. The new President's two counselors literally did not know where all the Men's Rooms were.

Haig was in control because he knew the rooms, controlled the internal machinery and had the loyalty of almost everyone in the building; he had hired or promoted most of the men and women there. The chief of staff managed the schedule-making procedure—no Ford person knew how it was done—and almost every day began with an hour-long Ford-Haig meeting to plan the President's routine. After a few days of informal hustle and confusion, all memos to the President were routed through Haig—just as they had been under Nixon. Within two weeks, internal distribution of the memos was controlled by a Haig list; members of the Ford transition team couldn't even find out what decisions the President was being asked to make.

"Action memos"—the basic policy instruments of the President of the United States—were pouring through the Oval Office. Sixteen went through Haig to Ford on August 14 alone, as White House holdovers energetically went about the business of locking the new man into Nixon administration politics.

The cover sheet on the decision package that day listed many of the principal domestic issues facing the country: "1. Agriculture-Environmental and Consumer Protection Appropriation Act, 1975; 2. Campaign Reform Legislation; 3. Cargo Preference Legislation; 4. Consumer Protection Agency Legislation; 5. ERDA (Energy Research and Development Administration) Status of legislation to create; 6. Freedom of Information Act Amendments (HR 12471); 7. Juvenile Delinquency Legislation (s.821); 8. Mass Tran-

77

sit; 9. National Health Insurance; 10. OEO Community Action Program; 11. Omnibus Housing Bill of 1974; 12. Private Pension Reform Legislation—Employee Retirement Income Security Act, HR 2; 13. Safe Drinking Water Legislation; 14. Surface Mining; 15. Veterans Education Bill; 16. White House Authorization Bill."

The form of the memos was the substance of Presidential decision-making.

MEMORANDUM FOR THE PRESIDENT

FROM: KEN COLE

SUBJECT: *OEO Community Action Program*

Background:

The Nixon Administration, from 1969 on, considered direct Federal support of the Community Action Program inappropriate. They first considered folding this program into Urban Community Development Revenue Sharing, but that option was subsequently dropped. The budgets for 1974 and 1975 then proposed termination of OEO and Community Action.

Key Facts:

The Congress is considering bills which would either continue Community Action in a new, separate agency, or transfer it to HEW. (A transfer bill has passed the House 331-53.) State and local officials across the political spectrum strongly support Community Action as a Federal program. The Community Action appropriations authorization expired June 30, 1974, and the program currently operates under a Continuing Resolution. The basic authorization for the program itself expires June 30, 1975.

Current Position:

The Administration has proposed a bill to discontinue the program and authorize HEW to oversee the orderly phase-out of Community Action activities in 1975.

78

Options:

1. Support the House bill which would eliminate OEO and transfer Community Action to HEW.

   Pro — This would recognize the strong House sentiment for Community Action.

   Con — Would probably rule out any future chance of phasing out Community Action.

2. Support the House bill with an amendment providing Executive reorganization authority to break up Community Action within HEW at the end of 12 months.

   Pro — Would give you an opportunity to reassess the situation after one year.

   Con — It could be both difficult and unwise to move this program twice in such a short period of time.

3. Support Gaylord Nelson's proposal for a 12-month extension of OEO with reorganization authority at the end of the year.

   Pro — Would put the issue to rest for now and give us the opportunity for a better deal next year.

   Con — Would continue a crippled OEO for 12 months with the possibility Community Action would end up in HEW after all.

4. Indicate support for Javits' proposal for an independent community action agency within the Executive branch.

   Pro — Would be recognizing support for Community Action.

   Con — Such an agency could be more difficult to phase out than an HEW program.

5. Maintain opposition to any legislation to continue Federal support of Community Action.

79

Pro — Would be consistent with philosophy that Community Action is more properly a State/local program and save the Federal Government over $300 million.

Con — Veto may not be sustained.

Staff Views:

Ash   Option 5—maintain our current position of opposition "I don't have $300 million."

Timmons   Option 5—maintain opposition.

Recommendation:

I recommend we maintain opposition—for time being—we can always switch later.

Decision:

Option 1. _____
        2. _____
        3. _____
        4. _____
        5. _____   (Recommended by Ash, Timmons, Cole)

The President, as he did in virtually every case, initialed the recommended option. The recommenders were the architects of Nixon domestic policy—Roy Ash, director of the Office of Management and Budget; William Timmons, director of Congressional Relations under Nixon; and Ken Cole, John Ehrlichman's former assistant and successor as director of the Domestic Council. All three were listed by Ford's transition team as Nixon symbols who had to be dismissed if Ford hoped to establish credibility as more than a caretaker for the disgraced former President.

It is an interesting comment on the final months of the Nixon administration and the beginning of the Ford administration that several high-ranking Federal officials told me that they really did not notice much of a difference when Presidents changed. Government itself had been ignored by the preoccupied Nixon White House and high-level officials were essentially unaware of any Ford influence for months. "We were used to operating in a vacuum; this was just a bigger vacuum," said John Sawhill, the Federal Energy administrator, who was later pushed out, giving him the freedom to be quoted:

"When Nixon was in, I used to go Ken Rush [his economic counselor] and say here is the issue, this is what I'm going to do. After August 9, there really was no one to go to, it was just a void." In September, Sawhill called the President, and Ford called back after five days. "He invited me over to the White House a few days later, and when I got there, Rog Morton and Bill Simon were with the President, and we had a bull session. We didn't talk about any specifics, just about whether one day there would be a Cabinet-level Department of Natural Resources. It was very nice. Ford has an easy way about him." What Sawhill did not know was that Morton and Simon were plotting to get him fired, and they did not want to give the Energy administrator a chance to be alone with the President—Ford might get to like Sawhill.

Bull sessions and action memos were pretty much the business of the Oval Office in those days, according to men who were in and out. The OEO memorandum—two and a half pages with five options—was more complicated than most. Ford complained about that and said he preferred one-page decision memos with a simpler bottom line: Approve_____, Disapprove_____.

It is probably stating the obvious to point out that control over Presidential options is close to control of Presidential decisions. But the transition team, with William Scranton doing the talking, did point that out to Ford in several briefings. In a separate memo to him on the night before he took office, the team also warned of "a stream of memoranda from the Domestic Council and OMB" and advised him to be careful not to give Ash and Cole the authority to push their own policies through the executive branch.*

* The confusion in the White House concerning policy was evident a month later when Ford nominated Bert Gallegos as Director of the Office of Economic Opportunity. Asked at his Senate confirmation

Among the memoranda Ford approved in those days was a "speed-up program" for Project Independence, a Nixon program for reducing American oil consumption and increasing domestic petroleum production. Ford had never seen the blueprints for the project—they were kept from him as Vice-President by the same men who sent the memorandum into his office as President.

---

hearings what the Ford Administration's policy was on merging OEO into HEW, Gallegos said he didn't know, no one had told him, and he had never talked with the President.

PRESIDENT FORD scheduled his first press conference for August 28, his twentieth day in office. He spent more than ten hours preparing for the national telecast, the last two in separate dress rehearsals with staff members throwing out the toughest and meanest questions they could think of, including: "Mr. President, didn't you help hound Mr. Nixon from office for your own benefit?"

The twenty-seven questions asked in twenty-nine minutes by real reporters were more polite, and the conference was acclaimed a success, with great emphasis on the fact that Ford spoke in front of an open door in the East Room rather than before the blue drapes Nixon favored—"Plain Words Before An Open Door" said the *Time* headline. But if Ford was sunny as usual, there was something dark in the lines of questioning. Ten questions picked at the country's sagging, inflating economy; eleven were about Nixon and Watergate.

Helen Thomas of United Press International, the senior wire correspondent with traditional first-question privileges, asked: "Mr. President, do you agree with Governor Rockefeller that former President Nixon should have immunity from prosecution? And specifically, would you use your pardon authority if necessary?"

The answers to that and subsequent questions included these lines: "Now the expression made by Governor Rockefeller, I think, coincides with the general view and point of view of the American people. I subscribe to that point of view . . . In the last ten days or two weeks, I've asked for prayers for guidance on this very important point . . . In this situation I am the final authority . . . I am not ruling it out. It is an option and a proper option for any President . . . I said at the outset that *until the matter reaches me, I am not going to make any comment during the process of whatever charges are made.*"

"Until the matter reaches me" is part of the standard language of political evasion. Public officials use lines like that to buy time. The press, in general, saw no warning flags in Ford's words, and reports of the news conference indicated that the President would probably wait through months of court action before even considering the delicate business of possible clemency for his predecessor.

Eleven days later, on a Sunday, September 8, White House correspondents received early-morning phone calls summoning them for an important Presidential announcement. When the reporters began arriving at 9:30, television lights were being set up in the Oval Office, and at 11, the President sat behind his desk: "Ladies and gentlemen, I have come to a decision which I felt I should tell you and all of my fellow American citizens as soon as I was certain in my own mind and in my conscience that it is the right thing to do . . . Now, therefore, I, Gerald R. Ford, President of the United States, pursuant to the pardon power conferred upon me by Article II, Section 2, of the Constitution, have granted and by these presents do grant a full, free and absolute pardon unto Richard Nixon for all offenses against the United States which he, Richard Nixon, has committed or may have committed or taken part in during the period from January 20, 1969, through August 9, 1974."

Late that night, Ford picked up a telephone in his living

quarters and asked a White House switchboard operator if many calls were coming in. "It's very heavy, Mr. President," she said, "and kind of unfavorable."

4

The Ordinary Man

"If you once forfeit the confidence of your fellow citizens, you can never regain their respect and esteem. It is true that you may fool all of the people some of the time; you can even fool some of the people all of the time; but you can't fool all of the people all the time."

Abraham Lincoln

AN HOUR before President Ford had faced the cameras to announce the pardon, Jerry terHorst had walked into the Oval Office to hand his old friend and new boss a one-page letter in an envelope marked in red: "The President—Eyes Only."

TerHorst had not slept since learning of the pardon the morning before. After talking with his wife, Louise, for two hours, the press secretary had worked through the night, writing and rewriting a letter of resignation until a White House limousine picked him up at 6 A.M.: "Without doubt this is the most difficult decision I ever have had to make. I cannot find words to adequately express my respect and admiration for you . . . I must inform you that I cannot in good conscience support your decision to pardon former President Nixon before he has been charged with the commission of any crime. As your spokesman, I do not know how I could credibly defend that action in the absence of a like decision to grant absolute pardon to the young men who evaded Vietnam military service as a matter of conscience and the absence of pardons for former aides and associates of Mr. Nixon . . . Try as I can, it is impossible to conclude that the former President is more deserving of mercy than persons of lesser station in life whose offenses have had far less effect on our national well-being." *

Like Ford, terHorst could not break the habits of a lifetime—he had been a newspaperman for twenty-five years, a press secretary for only thirty days. But even in thirty days on the inside, terHorst had unknowingly passed along the lies of the men around the President to his old colleagues and friends. Two days before the pardon was announced, David Kraslow of the Cox Newspapers had gone to terHorst for confirmation of a tip that a lawyer working for the White House was at San Clemente, negotiating a pardon agreement. The press secretary checked the story with Philip Buchen, who had been named Ford's counsel, and Buchen said no, that Benton Becker, "a dear friend of the President's," was in San Clemente but was there only on a routine assignment to discuss the disposition of Nixon tapes and documents still in the White House. TerHorst transmitted the information to Kraslow and the Cox papers killed the story.

In the White House press room, terHorst was the new hero. Ford, Saturday's hero, was Sunday's bum. While the country's approval of the President dropped from 71 per cent to 50 per cent after the pardon, according to a Gallup poll commissioned by the New York *Times,* the press was less restrained, dropping Ford from near 100 to near zero. Reporters just

* The resignation was an extraordinary act. There is no tradition of resignation in protest in American government. In fact, a study published this year by Edward Weisband and Thomas M. Franck showed that there have been fewer than forty public resignations over principle in the U.S. government in the twentieth century. Almost without exception, the careers of the protest resigners were destroyed for violating the American ethic of loyalty and team play. After it was over, terHorst, whose career as a journalist was thriving, told me: "I very distinctly recall the moment I took my oath of office, and there was nothing in that oath that said I was working for the President of the United States and that I owed him my loyalty to the extent that I would do anything for him. My loyalty was pledged to the United States of America."

turned a full 180 degrees and began to pound Ford and his lousy English muffins.

Time magazine, one of the leaders of the charge of the press brigade toward instant greatness, retreated as aggressively: "Somewhat jesting earlier cracks about Ford's intellect were now reviewed in a more serious light. How could he have failed to perceive the ramifications—legal, political and moral—of his decision?"

The press is a child, essentially an immature institution. It's a lovable little thing, distracted by bits of color and light, eager and irresponsible, honest in its simple way. And it has trouble concentrating on more than one thing at a time.

Those of us who are part of it know all this, but we forget it sometimes—most times, actually. After it was over, one of us, David Broder of the Washington *Post,* summed it up rather well: "It was an emotional backlash to a self-induced high. The press was betrayed, not by the real Gerald Ford, but by the mythical super-President created by the press's own artifice."

It hadn't been hard to romanticize Ford after the disgraceful Nixon exit, and it may have been necessary—Tocqueville had long ago defined the essential political role of the American press as "the maintenance of public tranquility." In a traumatic transition, the new President needed all the help he could get, and reporters, after all, are Americans who love their country. The history of journalism, or the journalism of journalism, is punctuated with incidents in which reporters put citizenship above profession—James Reston of the New York *Times* not reporting his knowledge of American U-2 surveillance of the globe; John Scali of ABC acting as a secret courier between Russian and U.S. diplomats during the Cuban missile crisis; Seymour Topping of the *Times* reporting conversations with Chinese Communist diplomats to the State Department but not to *Times'* readers.

The trumpeted adversary relationship between reporters and the people they cover has always been more sound than fury—

although the press did become more adverse and smarter and tougher when they were exposed to the official Southern injustice of the civil rights days, and then to the official lying of Vietnam and Nixon.

There is, however, inevitable tension between press and politicians; they are forced to work and march together, but they have different jobs and hear different drummers. Tension may be mistaken for struggle, but it does not necessarily make adversaries; in this case it only makes press and politicians loving and hating partners in a marriage of necessity. And the press knows its place in the partnership—at the White House that place is at ground level and below in a press area sunken in the West Wing. It's generally a pretty tame place, too. There is something Pavlovian about a room with two small plastic stars in the corner—when the stars in the briefing room light up, it means the "lid" is on, no more news will be handed out that day. Reporters may go home then, and they do. White House correspondents cannot leave the press area and go into any other part of the White House without permission. It is not hard to tell who is really in control.

Ithiel de Sola Pool, the Massachusetts Institute of Technology political scientist, put it this way: "Unless one can prove that there are circumstances under which a free and critical press will help sustain national consensus and rally the nation in support of national goals, then no argument for a free press will save it in practice. No nation will indefinitely tolerate a freedom of the press that serves to divide the country and to open the floodgates of criticism against the freely chosen government that leads it . . . If the press is the government's enemy, it is the free press that will end up being destroyed."

The press, in reality, is generally uncomfortable even with the appearance of being government's enemy, an enemy of the people. That is part of the reason that newspapers and networks will always fall back on Constitutional arguments (the First Amendment) when they are temporarily in opposition to the governors, as if they, too, were part of the government.

94

Nor does it seem to matter how unpopular the governor of the moment might be. The press is very, very careful to remember the emperor is always clothed. When President Nixon was sinking to his lowest point during his last months in power, he traveled to Houston for a news conference in front of an audience of broadcast executives who reacted with some applause and boos when one of his more famous antagonists, Dan Rather of CBS, rose to ask a question. "Are you running for something?" Nixon asked in an awkward attempt to be funny.

"No sir, Mr. President. Are you?" Rather said. Later, among themselves, reporters almost unanimously agreed that Rather had gone too far, inflated his own role; after all, he was speaking to the President of the United States. CBS apparently agreed that Rather had crossed some kind of line, and the controversial correspondent soon found himself unhappily transferred to vague duties in New York.

The press also keeps clothes on the emperor's men. On August 20, President Ford exercised his power under the 25th Amendment and nominated former governor Nelson Rockefeller of New York as his new Vice-President. The White House loudspeakers announced that Mr. Ford's counselor, Robert Hartmann, would brief the press on the procedure used in selecting Rockefeller. For two hours, sixty reporters waited in the press area until Hartmann arrived and began slowly walking through the briefing room slapping reporters on the back.

Those slapped could tell, or smell, that Hartmann had been drinking—at least I could. When he began to talk, slowly, sometimes unintelligibly, it was obvious that he had been drinking a lot. But for thirty-one minutes, the White House press corps asked polite questions, and that night, network correspondents appeared on the White House lawn, repeating scraps of Hartmann's muddled sentences after the words "A high White House source told me that . . ."

The White House press briefing, scheduled each weekday

for 11 A.M., is the fount of most of the news the American people get about their government. That is a terrible comment, because the President is not the government. It is the press that often makes one man appear to be the government, or even to be running the government, which Gerald Ford was certainly not doing in the late summer of 1974.

"The common-sense view seems to escape us in Washington," said David Broder. "We are congenitally incapable of getting it out of our heads that the President is just another politician who ought to be viewed with tolerant skepticism as a human being, and be judged over some reasonable length of time on the basis of the inevitable successes and failures of public policy for which he can be held to account. Instead we seem determined to take him with us on a roller coaster ride— elevating him to paragon status for no good reason and then condemning him utterly when, in our view, he makes his first mistake.

"Above all else, we seem unable to broaden our view beyond the White House and let people know the government is larger and more complex than one man. The result of that tunnel vision is that far worse examples of irresponsible behavior go by unheeded and unchecked every day in Washington than those Presidential aberrations that preoccupy us."

So, while the marble buildings along the Capital's boulevards are covered by a few sweaty men and women, thirty or fifty or a hundred reporters crowd into the White House briefing room each morning and wait. They usually wait an hour or an hour and a half before the President's press secretary, a $42,500-a-year public relations man, steps behind a small podium and apologizes for being late again. He carries a large, black loose-leaf binder, the "briefing book," prepared over the preceding three hours after consultation with the President and his senior advisers. Ronald Nessen, a former NBC correspondent who became Ford's second press secretary, estimated that the White House press corps' questions elicit 15 to 20 per cent of the information in the book each day—information the one man at the top of a huge bureaucracy has and has decided to reveal if anyone asks. "It's not my job to tell them if they don't ask," said Nessen, who gloried in his transformation from asker to asked.

Nessen's job is to keep the White House press corps occupied, dumb and happy. He runs an adult day-care center. If he were not there doling out a daily ration of front-page headlines and ninety-second television spots, all those reporters, many of them talented men and women, might be prowling around the government talking to people in, say, the State or Defense departments, people who know what is going on.

The "spokesman" is a particularly insidious device developed by politicians and public relations men with the lazy acquiescence of people like me. Nessen shields Ford, as other spokesmen shield other officials accountable to the public, and controls a flow of pseudoinformation, mixed truths, half-truths, evasions and, occasionally, lies, through the press. Government, governed and press might be better served by a system of fairly regular Presidential press conferences, a daily pile of Presidential statements that could be picked up by a copy boy, and some credible "no comments." Politics and government, like most businesses, have built-in levels of honesty and dishonesty. The ironic thing about Ford's constant professions of candor and openness is that what he really means is that he tries to be as honest as a politician can. He and all other politicians and salesmen are in the information-deploying, image-making business. Their stock-in-trade is favorable partial truths. The timing of information release and the amount released is critical to them. It is the business of President Johnson denying newspaper reports that he was considering sending as many as 225,000 troops to Vietnam—he was not actually lying because the number was 200,000. Buchen acted like an amateur in lying to terHorst; a professional would have said only that Benton Becker was in San Clemente about the tapes, a partial truth.

Those partial truths are at the core of American government's credibility problems. The public was bound to find out that Johnson and Buchen were not telling the whole truth. Even if they said "no comment," no one would have believed them because "no comment" has become a confirmation that a story is true. Now officials only refuse to comment when stories are embarrassing; perhaps we would all be better off if they steadfastly said nothing if they couldn't tell reasonable truth. And, if a few politicians ever began saying "no comment" to stories that were either favorable or untrue, reporters would soon take those two words seriously.

As it is, nobody believes anybody, least of all spokesmen, and the White House continues to dole out news, usually one story a day, basically because reporters only want one story a day.

Reporting is a kind of prolonged adolescence—journalism is one of the few businesses where lack of commitment and absence of conviction are considered high virtues—and the daily reporter is after instant gratification. He only needs one story with his by-line to appear within a few hours. Anything more is work without reward—most newspapers do not put by-lines on a reporter's second story, and second stories or any other complications are anathema to television and radio. The real work of the briefing is the pinning down of that one story, which is often announced at the beginning of the briefing by the press secretary, as it was on August 15, when Jerry ter Horst announced that the State Department was urging Turkey to comply with United Nations cease-fire resolutions after the Turkish invasion of Cyprus.

"Is it the United States or the President personally who is strongly urging compliance?" a reporter asked.

"Both," terHorst answered.

"Can we say today that 'The President strongly urges etc., etc.?' "

"Precisely, Ralph."

"That is the point of it?"

"That is the point of it," terHorst concluded.

The rest of the briefing can usually be characterized as referral and housekeeping. Referrals are the White House's aggravating ritual for avoiding comment without refusing comment. The press secretary refers persistent questioners to another agency—the Defense Department, for instance—then that agency refers back to the White House until a reporter forgets about the whole thing or goes digging for information himself; it is almost always the former.

Housekeeping—known in the trade, as in most trades, as "chickenshit"—takes up a lot of time because a press secretary has enormous control over the daily lives and comfort of White House correspondents. Reporters are people with the usual run of personal and family responsibilities, and a press secretary can make a man's life easy or miserable by telling him, for example, whether or not the President will be in Washington, Colorado or Tokyo the next week, because the correspondent is going to have to be in the same place. In Lyndon Johnson's time, the President would take off for Texas on an hour's notice, leaving reporters to telephone wives and husbands to explain why they wouldn't be home for the next three days. Real life goes on—one of the reasons that Ford's first days in the White House were reported even more superficially than usual was that experienced Washington reporters began taking weeks of vacation time accumulated during the daily overtime crises of the Watergate months.

So on August 14, the President's press secretary and fifty of the nation's better-known reporters were reduced to dialogue like this:

"Jerry, the Japanese Foreign Office has announced today that the President will visit Japan at the earliest possible date convenient to both countries. Can you tell us about that please? . . . Why was it left to a foreign office to announce a Presidential trip?"

"We are announcing it now . . . If I may go on background, there, and not for attribution, it would appear that a trip by President Ford to Japan would occur before late November or early December."

When the daily briefing ends, one of the plastic stars on the wall usually lights up, signaling a "temporary lid," and the ladies and gentlemen of the press are free to go to lunch for an hour, secure in the knowledge that no news will be handed out until the stars dim again. There are no Washington briefings when the President travels. The whole show just takes to the road with the press secretary and his staff acting as guides and social directors for fifty to one hundred newspaper, magazine and television tourists, handing out hotel keys, schedules and speech transcripts like preprinted postcards for the folks back home.

White House correspondents, at home or traveling, rarely get within fifty feet of the President of the United States. They are usually politely herded by Secret Service men into roped enclosures at the sides of airport runways or banquet halls, or they are a helicopter ride behind the President, listening to his voice on a loudspeaker system hooked to a room miles away. The reporters closest to the Presidential body itself are "the pool," three to six reporters selected on a rotating basis to follow in the helicopter behind the President's, or a car four cars behind his, or in a smaller velvet-roped enclosure in a smaller room, or in the isolated press section of Air Force One, the President's Boeing 707. During his first thirty days, Ford won great praise for openness by twice walking back to the plane's press section, shirtsleeves rolled up and Scotch in hand, to chat with pool reporters. But when heavy criticism of the new President began, pool reporters' requests for face-to-face talk regularly were greeted with a press secretary-delivered "No."

Like children, the press is not always to be taken seriously, but it does have to be constantly watched. In *The Making of the President 1972,* Theodore H. White (among others, including President Nixon) argued that the power of the press was increasing in post-World War II, television-glued America.

"The power of the press in America is a primordial one. It sets the agenda for public discussion," White wrote. "It determines what people will talk and think about—an authority that in other nations is reserved for tyrants, priests, parties and mandarins."

Most working reporters would disagree with that, arguing that government and "the people" set the agenda, whether it is the government deciding to act in Vietnam or black people deciding to demonstrate for civil rights. A real test of power would have been for the press to ignore things like racial unrest. Reporters prefer to see themselves as only observers— "Hey, I didn't say *anything,* I just wrote what he said." That attitude is part of a life style devoted to avoiding responsibility and much of the business is about just that—avoiding responsibility. It might be going too far to say that the press is essentially and inherently an irresponsible institution. But most reporters and most of the editors I have known are happily irreverent to the point of nonresponsibility, if not irresponsibility, and among themselves, that self-selected band of brothers and some sisters are proud of it.

The rhetoric of the press, both inner- and outer-directed, is antipower and, implicitly, antiresponsibility—we do not accept the responsibility for the impact of our work. There are exceptions, but most reporters will insist that they are not interested in the impact of what they write or what they say on television or radio; and if they are interested in influence, it is influence among their bosses, the editors, and their peer group, other reporters.

And they believe their own rhetoric about themselves probably because it is substantially true. Take two men from the National Broadcasting Company, men who would certainly be considered among the most powerful in American journalism—commentator David Brinkley and Richard Wald, the president of NBC News.

"There are numerous countries in the world where the politicians have seized absolute power and muzzled the press," said Brinkley. "There is no country in the world where the press has seized absolute power and muzzled the politicians."

101

"We, print and television, look powerful right now," said Wald, a former managing editor of the New York *Herald Tribune,* as Gerald Ford assumed the Presidency. "But I think the power of the press is roughly a constant. It becomes impressive when things are happening in the society—and things are certainly happening right now—and when there are new developments in the technology of communication. Television is obviously the technological change, but its impact seems remarkably similar to the impact of the rotary press in the late nineteenth century. Circulation of news exploded, and there was a great outcry about the power of the 'mass press.' It was a time of change in society—the Industrial Revolution—it was not a happy event having the problems of the day stated so widely; papers like the New York *Sun* were regularly accused of inflaming the masses."

It is not that the press has no power; it has a great deal. But it is not an institution consciously and consistently dedicated to accumulating the exercise of control over other institutions or other people's lives. It is, in fact, diverse, cantankerous, rarely consistent and often unconscious about the power it has, not unlike a bunch of kids throwing firecrackers around the Metropolitan Museum of Art.

The value system of the American press can be rationalized by insiders and is widely misunderstood by outsiders. Reporters are after *stories.* Human considerations, ethics and other restraints have a way of being hurdled in that process. In late 1974, when Yasir Arafat, the head of the Palestine Liberation Organization, arrived in New York to speak at the United Nations, a reporter from Hsinhua, the Chinese news agency, asked Michael Berlin, the U.N. correspondent of the New York *Post,* what he thought would be the best possible result of the Arafat appearance. "I told him I wanted an assassination on the floor of the General Assembly about a half-hour before deadline. He thought I was kidding."

The press in heat is awesome and more than a little scary, as George McGovern learned during his Presidential campaign in 1972, Nixon found out in 1973, and Ford was reminded on September 8.

The new President had twenty-five years of experience in dealing with reporters, and he had slowly learned to manipulate them, to try to use them for his own ends. Part of Ford's development as a national politician was learning to restrain his instinct for direct response. Some politicians seem to be born learning to ramble on without saying anything, but Ford had to learn the hard way to evade and ignore leading and loaded questions. It is a sad comment on the evolution of American leadership, but the development of the technology of instant national communication has been paralleled by increasing sophistication in political noncommunication. Public questions today are electronically projected as crises so quickly that overexposed politicians feel compelled to speak out before they understand the questions, their implications or the public temper. So the politicians who scramble to network television cameras each day in Washington—senators can sometimes be seen jogging toward the press galleries late in the day—have learned the essential techniques of noncommunicative verbosity.

The rhetoric of the least-objectionable-alternative politicians was summed up by Agar Jaicks, a television producer who knows enough about politics to be San Francisco County Democratic chairman: "People who speak out these days on questions that involve the stability of the country are rarely those who seek elective office. Campaigners don't dare venture into saying something challenging or new. The people of courage and intelligence who will try to articulate their views in a persuasive manner are not the conventional politicians. They are the leaders of new causes emerging from the people. When we bring politicians in [to the studio], they don't really have that much to say that is new. They talk in clichés. The contrast is devastating."

But if Ford's words rarely dazzled reporters, his friendliness warmed them. As minority leader and Vice-President he gen-

103

erally got a good press, a lot of it just because he was a nice guy. He liked reporters and they liked him. And don't think that is not reflected in front-page stories and on the nightly news. He also worked at flattering the press. As President he invited newsmen like David Broder of the Washington *Post,* James Reston of the New York *Times* and Howard K. Smith of ABC in for White House lunches. Not for interviews, either —he did the interviewing, asking them what they thought was going on in the country, what they thought he should be doing.

Ford learned you can play the press like a mighty Wurlitzer, and the one area in the White House where he moved quickly and decisively was in setting up his own public relations apparatus on top of the $400 million a year information machine of the Federal government. That $400 million for information offices, officers and mimeograph machines is more than double the combined news budgets of the three television networks, Associated Press, United Press International and the country's ten largest newspapers.*

By the end of his first hundred days in the White House, Ford had expanded the Nixon public relations staff to the point that one out of five of the 250 men and women reporting directly to the President and his senior staff were working on public relations. Among other helpers, Ford had a $40,000-a-year joke writer, Bob Orben, who used to do the same thing for Jack Paar and Red Skelton, and a $40,000 personal television director, Robert Mead, who used to be Dan Rather's White House producer for CBS. Mead, along with directing cameras, picked the new President's TV shirts and ties, held up signs that said "stand up," "sit down," and "change cam-

* The $400 million, almost all of it spent in the executive branch under Presidential control, is an incomplete and conservative figure. It was compiled in 1969 by the Associated Press, which found among other things that the executive public information budget was more than the combined operating budget of Congress and the Federal judiciary. The director of the Office of Economic Opportunity, for instance, had forty-six full-time public relations assistants.

104

eras," prohibited Ford from eating for two hours before television appearances to prevent on-camera belches, and gently pushed the President forward at the precise moment he was supposed to move when the announcer said, "Ladies and gentlemen, the President of the United States."

ON TELEVISION that Sunday afternoon, September 8, Gerald Ford's taped image said he was granting the pardon "to heal the wounds throughout the United States." On those terms, the decision was a monumental misjudgment, an act of extraordinary political stupidity. What he had done was to reopen the wounds of Watergate; he had destroyed his own capability to reunite the nation.

Mistrust bound us together again and the viciousness of the past two years resurfaced. The Chicago *Tribune* editorially complained of "a sour smell" again in the White House, *Newsweek* said Ford had "embraced the demon of Watergate" and, for the first time, the new President was booed as he traveled to North Carolina the day after he announced the pardon and saw signs that read, "Justice Died 9/8/74." Within a month, like Nixon and Johnson before him, Ford sometimes had to leave the halls where he spoke by way of back doors and basements; he used the basement exit at the University of Vermont while at the front door 500 students alternately chanted "No pardon! No pardon!" and "Eat shit! Eat shit!"

The White House again seemed a secret, guarded place, somehow separate from 200 million daily American lives.

And, again, it was a desperate place, with the President and the President's men leaking hypothetical and fabricated "inside" stories of why Ford acted—he had drastic information on Nixon's health, there was a hidden reason that would someday be revealed—but the outrage could not be calmed so easily. In fact, it became worse as second readings made it clear that Nixon had avoided admitting guilt, only conceding "mistakes," and that Ford had approved an agreement allowing the former President to destroy his damning Oval Office tapes in five years.*

Ford, for at least twenty-four hours on September 9 and 10, seemed as out of touch with American reality as Nixon had been a couple of months earlier. His temporary "spokesman," Deputy Press Secretary Jack Hushen, who used to "speak" for Attorney General John Mitchell, told the daily press briefing the day after the Nixon pardon that the President had authorized him to say that pardons were "under study" for all Watergate defendants and convicts, forty former Nixon men.

"Jack, are you aware of the impact of what you have just said is going to have on the American people?" asked Peter Lisagor of the Chicago *Daily News*. Hushen said he understood.

All hell broke loose again—at least newspaper, television, telegraph and telephone protest broke. For a full day, Ford refused comment, his aides refused comment, his spokesman did not speak. A reasonable man could only conclude that

---

* The tapes agreement negotiated by the White House and Nixon was the second attempt by the Ford administration to maximize the former President's control over the damaging recordings. The Senate reacted to the September 8 agreement by first passing a Sense of the Senate Resolution protesting the planned transfer to San Clemente, then passing a bill making the tapes the property of the Federal government. Finally, on November 11, the White House and the Justice Department filed motions in Federal Court agreeing to placing the tapes and Nixon documents under the control of the Office of the Special Prosecutor.

108

the President really was considering letting everyone go free. Then, after twenty-four hours of howling outside the gates, poor Jack Hushen was trotted out again to say it was all a misunderstanding. He said he had been quoted out of context —not true. He said the press had misunderstood him—not true. He said he must have misunderstood the President— possible, but then why did Ford wait twenty-four hours to straighten him out? He said what he really meant was that the entire Federal pardon policy was what was "under study" —not true, inquiries revealed.

Hushen, of course, knew nothing about pardons or the pardon. He was just "the spokesman," sent out to keep reporters busy and Americans unsure. No one in the White House knew anything basic about the Nixon pardon except Gerald Ford and maybe Alexander Haig. Those two had discussed pardon possibilities for hours in the week before Nixon resigned—and, at the least, Haig is a perceptive man. Some sources in the old Nixon White House said that after those Ford-Haig meetings there was not much discussion of Presidential pardon. It was taken for granted that Ford would take care of Nixon, and high-level White House discussion in the final Nixon days focused on strategies to get the tapes into Nixon's personal possession.

In the White House the subject of pardon came up on August 9, Ford's first day in office, when terHorst was asked about it during his premier briefing. The new press secretary had not talked to the new President about the possibility of a pardon, but he decided to wing it, referring reporters to Ford's old statement that the American people would never stand for it.

The next morning, August 10, terHorst showed Ford a transcript of what he had told the reporters the day before. Ford glanced at it and said, "That's okay."

TerHorst left the Oval Office with Al Haig, who turned on him outside the door and angrily asked what right he had to try to commit Ford on the possibility of a pardon. There was never any doubt inside the White House about where Haig and the other old Nixon assistants stood on clemency —they were for it, and they were for maximum comfort for their old boss. Among the Nixon-staff-prepared decision memos Haig pushed across Ford's desk was one seeking congressional appropriation of $850,000 to cover the former President's transition to private life, his Federal pension and other expenses for an eleven-month period. Ford initialed it on August 28. The $850,000, however, was $300,000 more than former President Lyndon Johnson received for an eighteen-month transition, and congressional committees immediately challenged Ford's generosity, cutting the appropriation by more than half.

Haig sometimes appeared quite discreet when the pardon process actually began in the White House—that was on August 30, when Ford told Buchen that he was disturbed by the pardon questions at the August 28 news conference and wanted research on precedents for issuing pardons before a person was indicted, tried or convicted. Buchen later said that he had no doubt at that moment that the President had already decided to issue the pardon, that "he was just looking for a way to do it."

The official explanations of why the President pardoned Nixon when he did concentrate on his reaction to the questions at the press conference. White House assistants indicated that Ford was surprised by the questions and then began thinking seriously about an early pardon. But his own words and those of Nelson Rockefeller strongly indicate those explanations were misleading. Ford himself reacted at the press conference by talking about two weeks of prayer on the subject, and the question he responded to was prompted by Rockefeller statements favoring clemency. Although Rockefeller would not talk about it later, it is almost inconceivable that he would speak out on a subject that sensitive and exclusively Presidential without signals from Ford.

When a few very small and very secret meetings were held

110

in the Oval Office after August 30 to "consider" a pardon, Haig sometimes left, saying, "Perhaps it would be better if I excused myself on this." Hartmann, who argued against the pardon, was not impressed by such obvious discretion—he was sure Haig knew the decision was already made. Others were suspicious because Haig was noticeably less discreet in advocating that tapes and records be turned over to Nixon and that Ford continue to resist turning those materials over to Special Prosecutor Leon Jaworski as a matter of "executive privilege."

On Ford's instructions, Buchen contacted Jaworski and reported back that Nixon was "absolutely certain" to be indicted for obstruction of justice and that the special prosecutor estimated it would be nine months to a year before he went to trial. Benton Becker, who had investigated Justice William O. Douglas for Ford five years earlier, was dispatched to San Clemente to work out the details of the pardon and tapes agreement. He was back in Washington on Saturday, September 7. Ford began rehearsing for his television statement.

The entire process had been completed in ten days and in unbroken secrecy. After taping the statement in the Oval Office and signing the pardon proclamation, Ford was driven to the Burning Tree Club in suburban Maryland for a round of golf with Mel Laird. He was there when the statement was broadcast to the American people.

PRAYER is not a word that Gerald Ford uses lightly. Although thousands and thousands of words—true, untrue and contradictory—came officially and unofficially out of the White House to explain why Ford pardoned Nixon, the most important were the few that came directly from the new President.

"In the last ten days or two weeks, I've asked for prayers for guidance on this very important point," said Ford, a Charismatic Christian and prayer breakfast regular, when he was asked about clemency at his August 28 news conference.

In announcing the pardon eleven days later, he said: "The Constitution is the supreme law of our land, and it governs our actions as citizens. Only the laws of God, which govern our consciences, are superior to it . . . Theirs [the Nixon family's] is an American tragedy [and] someone must write an end to it. I have concluded that only I can do that. And if I can, *I must* . . . As a man, my first consideration will always be to be true to my own convictions and my own conscience . . . I do believe with all my heart and mind and spirit that I, not as President, but as a humble servant of God, will receive justice without mercy if I fail to show mercy."

"*I must*" do this, Ford told the American people. I tend to believe those words were literally true. The decision was between Gerald Ford and his God, and his painfully personal rhetoric reflected personality and psychological pressures that made pardon inevitable. The Lord may have had a bit of help from Al Haig and the political judgment that it was better to get the inevitable political controversy over before the 1976 elections, but Ford, almost certainly, consciously or unconsciously, had decided to pardon Nixon before he became President on August 9, no matter what the consequences. Gerald R. Ford, Jr., did it because of who he is—and he probably would have done it if he knew for certain it would destroy his Presidency.

Gerald R. Ford, Jr., is Leslie Lynch King, Jr. He was born Leslie King in Omaha, Nebraska, in 1913. His father, a wool dealer, and his mother, Dorothy King, were divorced soon after he was born, and the mother and her infant son moved to Grand Rapids. When the boy was two years old, Dorothy King married Gerald R. Ford, Sr., a paint salesman. Ford adopted the boy, and his name was legally changed to Gerald R. Ford, Jr.

Jerry Ford, called "Junie" in those days, was seventeen years old, working behind the counter in Skourgis's Restaurant across the street from the South High School in Grand Rapids, when a man he had never seen before walked into the restaurant, watched him for a while, then said: "Leslie, I'm your father." He learned, for the first time, that he was an adopted son.*

There is a small literature on the psychology of adopted sons. They can tend to be, in the language of the profession,

* Ford, at different times, has given interviewers slightly different versions of this incident. He has said, at least once, that he actually learned he was adopted about a year before Leslie King walked in. He has also said on some occasions that the incident had no particular impact, and that it was "an interesting experience," and at other times that he was bitter for years about the apparent affluence of his real father, King, compared with the hard times of his family, the Fords.

114

"eternally grateful" to the father figure who freely took them in. They look to be the "favored son," the good boy wanting to please the adoptive father and father figures. They try to be nice to most people, perhaps fearing rejection more than most of us. And through their lives, they tend to subconsciously seek out other father figures.*

Has Ford searched for father figures? Possibly. He seems to have exaggerated and romanticized his association with the late Senator Arthur Vandenberg, who was also from Grand Rapids and who personally and politically disliked Representative Bartel Jonkman, the isolationist Republican Ford defeated in a primary in 1948 on his way to Congress. Although Ford often refers to Vandenberg's "sponsorship" of his career, there is no mention of Ford's name in Vandenberg's voluminous papers and diaries at the University of Michigan and there is no linking of their names in old files of Grand Rapids newspapers.

And Nixon? Ford almost idolized the Californian who came to Congress two years before him, and often talked of the "greatness" of Nixon, even when Nixon seemed down and out in the mid-1960's. In those days, Ford was fond of telling people that he kept in touch with Nixon—"He calls me and checks in with me, sometimes from pay phones at airports." Then, of course, President Nixon made Jerry Ford Vice-President and President of the United States—not a small inheritance to be grateful for.

Many people in politics respected Richard Nixon's abilities, but Ford was one of the few who talked about *liking* Nixon. But then, it is part of Ford's personality and charm to like almost everybody.

He places a very, very high value on friendliness and niceness. In an interview after Ford met Soviet Chairman Leonid

* I have no psychological training more formal than what you get being a reporter for fifteen years. In preparing this section, I consulted several psychiatrists and psychologists, all of whom asked not to be identified because of professional strictures.

115

Brezhnev for the first time, *Newsweek* editors asked Ford this question: "It has been suggested that you and Mr. Brezhnev have certain similarities in personality. How do you think he would do as a politician in this country?"

"I think he would do very well," Ford answered. "I was impressed with him. He is a strong person. He has some qualities that I like in a person. He is very friendly.

"And none of the experiences I have had with him indicate that he is a person who is mean or vindictive. None of that attitude at all. He was firm in what he wanted, and yet he could understand our point of view.

"He is very pleasant to be with. Very enjoyable, both not only when we were negotiating, but in the lunchroom and the automobile ride we took at the end where we spent an hour driving around Vladivostok, where I sat with him in the back seat. Very pleasant, very amiable in his discussions, very generous in the way he talks."

That is probably close to the way Ford sees himself. Certainly his Brezhnev description is fairly close to the way other people see Ford. After the first one hundred days of the Ford administration, the Washington *Post* assigned a team of reporters to spend six weeks interviewing people who knew Ford and had worked with him as President. The *Post* team came back to report:

"Senators and congressmen, Cabinet officers and State Department officials, White House aides and private counselors, political friends and foes—all strikingly agree about the Ford they see. The words used to describe him . . . form this abbreviated assessment:

"Positive traits: Warm. Honest. Generous. Loyal. Clear-eyed. Earnest. Sincere. Plain in manner and expression. Comfortable. Self-confident. A hard worker. A man of character, good sense, prudence and decency.

"Negative traits: Slow, plodding, pedestrian, unimaginative. Nonintellectual, lacks conceptual ability. Doesn't want change. Poorly staffed. Out of touch with people he needs to talk

116

with. Spread too thin. Does not use time wisely. Lacks sense of communications. Inarticulate."

The lists, basically from Ford's friends, seemed so negative that *Post* editors debated whether it was fair to publish it so early in the accidental administration. The reporters who did the interviews argued, successfully, that the list was a basic portrait of the man and was not likely to change with time.

I would add a few characterizations to those lists: Decisive. A little vain. Stubborn. Ignorant.

Because Ford seemed hesitant on advice to clean out the Nixon White House, he was quickly labeled as an indecisive President. But to many of the people who worked with him, it became apparent that the opposite was true—he had decided not to do it and was not going to be pressured into throwing anyone out. "Put yourself in my place, Barb," he told Barber Conable, one of many friends urging him to clean out the old Nixon hands. "I don't have a lot of high-powered associates to call on. The very people I'd have to replace are the ones who would have to screen their replacements. I have to run a functioning government."

Some thought he was too decisive—impetuous, almost impulsive. "He just jumps to conclusions and nobody can shake him," said a friend. "He doesn't think things through or he acts without enough information—the Douglas impeachment, the things he said on the war, the pardon, his decision that a gasoline tax was bad, there's a pattern."

He liked making decisions, it satisfied his work ethic and maybe his vanity, too. Hugh Carey, the governor of New York, who served with Ford in Congress, was shocked the first time he dealt with President Ford after Northeastern governors protested higher U.S. tariffs on imported oil. "Swashbuckling" was the word Carey used to describe the President's manner. "His attitude was sort of 'See what I did!'" Carey said, adding that the President told them: "I had to do something, so I did it."

117

Look at me! He liked being President. He liked being the center of attention, the focus of Kennerly's camera and all the others. There was always a golden-boy quality to Ford's life—young photographs of him with full blond hair and easy grins show that—from football star to four years as a part-time male model in New York to the strong, straight pictures of himself in his uniform as a Navy lieutenant commander, pictures he was still handing out five years after the war ended.

The Ford stubbornness was instant legend inside the White House: "I'm going!" ended a conversation with advisers suggesting he might want to postpone scheduled foreign travel and vacations while he was using crisis language to describe the American economy. He warned White House people who didn't know him well not to come back to him with their arguments after he had made a decision. His conversations on gasoline taxes were punctuated with phrases like "over my dead body."

Then there were vetoes. When Ford took a position on legislation before the 93rd Congress, and Congress then passed a bill that did not particularly fit his particulars, he vetoed it. That is not the way it is usually done. Ford vetoed more bills in three months (15) than Nixon had in eighteen months (12). And Ford had a higher percentage of vetoes overridden—four of fifteen with the vote to override reaching 398 to 7 once in the House of Representatives—than any President since Franklin Pierce had lost five of nine veto tests in the 1850's.

The new President who wanted a "marriage" with Congress was dissipating his veto power—that warning came from friends like Conable and John Rhodes, the Arizona congressman who succeeded him as Republican leader in the House. After Ford had been clobbered in veto fights over extensions of the Vocational Rehabilitation Act and Freedom of Information Act, Rhodes cautioned Ford that he was making it look too easy and routine to override Ford vetoes. "I have no choice but to be consistent and responsible," the President told his old friend.*

One of the consistencies about Ford has been that he does not know much; he has collected very little information over an adult lifetime of making speeches. And at least one woman spotted that in his very first political speech more than twenty-five years ago in Grand Rapids. The story has been told by Robert Kleiner, a Grand Rapids Democratic leader, who was one of Ford's earliest backers, along with other Democrats like Walter Reuther and Leonard Woodcock of the United Auto Workers, in the days when the city was so heavily Republican that there was no point in working for Democratic candidates.

"The first time Jerry made a speech in 1948, it was at the Fountain Street Church," Kleiner said. "Internationalism was very much the key issue. My mother was very much involved in United Nations work. I remember she came out after hearing Jerry talk, and she said to me and to Woodcock who was standing there with me: 'You gentlemen will be sorry. This young man is ignorant.'

"That is the way Jerry turned out. He's not stupid, he's not dumb. He's ignorant."

That is indeed the way it turned out. By 1975, Ford had become a great admirer of Harry Truman, another commoner President, but there was a revealing difference between the two plain-spoken Midwesterners. When Truman spoke of great and complicated issues, he used the first person singular —"I think . . . I want . . . I am . . . " Ford however, leans on phrasing like "My advisers . . . I have consulted many . . ." Truman was confident in his knowledge. Ford

* The vetoes were consistent with the recommendations on the legislation in the "Action" memos the President initialed in his first month or so in office. On the extension of the Vocational Rehabilitation Act for Vietnam veterans, Budget Director Roy Ash had recommended: "The Administration should continue to oppose the tuition assistance payment, the direct loans and the entitlement extension . . . would add $800 million to 1975 budget."

119

is not. Consequently, as President, Ford often found himself at the mercy of the knowledge of Henry Kissinger and of lesser assistants.

Ford's informational insecurity in many areas was quickly sensed within the web of power and ambition that spreads from the Oval Office. "My job is to protect the President from himself," said one of his top assistants in an unguarded moment of arrogance. "I'm here to override him if that's necessary."

His virtues and flaws were the traits of an ordinary man. After an Oval Office rehearsal with his gag writer, Bob Orben, Ford spoke lightly at the installation of Ronald Sarro of the Washington *Star* as the first male president of the formerly all-women's Washington Press Club. "I guess," Ford told the crowd, "it just proves that in America anyone can be President."

Anyone now was President of the United States. The President's joke echoed a comment by his old pastor in Grand Rapids, Reverend Donald Carey of Grace Episcopal Church: "Gerald Ford is a normal, decent, God-fearing man, but you can say that about a lot of people."

Ford celebrated ordinariness on the day after pardoning Nixon. In Pinehurst, North Carolina, for a round of golf at the opening of the World Golf Hall of Fame, the President said he loved to watch golf when he worked on Sundays. "I sit in front of the television and take a pile of work," he said, "and in between this shot and that shot, I try to concentrate."

FORD is an early riser and a newspaper reader, and becoming President did not change his daily routine. He got up each day between 5:30 and 6 A.M., after five to seven hours of sleep, and began reading the Washington *Post*. After exercises—a mile on a stationary bike, leg lifts with forty pounds strapped to his left leg, then twenty-five strapped to the right, twenty push-ups and twenty sit-ups—he read the New York *Times* while his breakfast was served by the U. S. Navy stewards who glided silently through his quarters and office plumping up cushions and pillows after each contact with a body.*

Because they knew his habits, many of the people around Ford tried to influence or manipulate him by using reporters and columnists to send the boss printed memos with his push-ups and orange juice—even unwanted and unassigned but tenacious Father McLaughlin was giving interviews saying Ford wanted him to stay.

* The President often looks through several other papers during a day, including the Washington *Star* and Grand Rapids *Press,* and is a regular reader of *Time* and *Newsweek* magazines. He told me he does not have time to read books—his press office later announced he read a book a month—and is generally familiar with the shows and characters of prime-time television. That last is not true of all politicians; they work long days and nights. Representative Elizabeth Holtzman of New York once asked a friend, "Who is Mary Tyler Moore?"

Much of the battle between Al Haig and Bob Hartmann was fought with leaks and lies planted in Ford's favorite papers and magazines. Not only was Ford listening to the two men's gripes about each other all day, he was reading Haig-inspired columns about Hartmann's administrative incompetence and slipping status in the Oval Office and Hartmann-inspired columns about Haig's subversion of Presidential directives.

Hartmann was winning the war of the whispers—among other things, as a former Washington bureau chief of the Los Angeles *Times*, he knew more reporters and more tricks than the former general. Almost any morning Ford could read that Haig really wanted to get back into the Army, or Haig could read that Ford really wanted him to quit but was too dependent and embarrassed to ask. Or they both could read intimations that Haig took his real orders in daily telephone conversations with Nixon in San Clemente. That was untrue, but Haig was beginning to realize that he might be nibbled to death if he did not find a graceful way out.

The White House was leaking like a sieve, but the President could not seem to stop it. He came to senior staff meetings and said that he did not like the leaks and he wanted them stopped. But he disliked personal confrontation and apparently did not face down the assistants he knew were responsible. Even after Haig left, it was still so bad that when Ford reacted to a leak campaign saying Treasury Secretary William Simon was on his way out by meeting with Simon and publicly pledging full Presidential confidence and support, columnists Rowland Evans and Robert Novak wrote in the *Post*: "Even if Simon is marked for dismissal in *a decision that has not yet filtered up to Mr. Ford*, it is definitely not Donald Rumsfeld's style to ease him out by anonymous leaks."

It is definitely not Evans and Novak's style to be subtle, and praising someone as a nonleaker is an ancient journalistic device to protect sources.

Rumsfeld's style is more subtle, and he had apparently been angling for Haig's job on his own terms from the moment

122

he heard rumors that Nixon was going to resign, and took the next plane to the United States from Paris, where he was vacationing from his post as U. S. ambassador to the North Atlantic Treaty Organization. He got the job, finally, on September 30. And he told at least one person it was on his terms—future appointment as secretary of State, Defense, or the Treasury.

But Rumsfeld had a way of saying a lot of different things to a lot of people—it is a political tactic, perfected, for instance, by Mel Laird, that makes it almost impossible to figure out what he is really after at any given time.

Rumsfeld had gone back to Brussels and his own NATO ambassadorship after the first couple of weeks of the Nixon-Ford transition, saying, for public consumption, he would never go back on the White House staff after what he learned as a counselor to Nixon. On September 4, with Hartmann and his troops putting out stories that Haig wanted to resign to become supreme commander of NATO armed forces, reporters spotted Rumsfeld back in Washington. He was meeting with Ford, and although the meetings were not on the President's handout schedule, anti-Haig White House staffers made sure word of the meeting got to the press room. Jerry terHorst was asked what was up.

Nothing, the press secretary said. "I am advised it's a routine mission." What about Haig? "There is no connection," terHorst said, repeating once again that Haig's tenure was "for the duration," whatever that meant.

None of that was true, of course. Rumsfeld was in talking about taking over as chief of staff and Ford had finally been convinced, by Bob Griffin and Charlie Goodell among others, that he was going to be President in name only until Haig was gone. But Haig still did not want to go and Ford was not about to push him. The President was both impressed with and dependent upon his chief of staff and had spent long hours resisting before concluding he had to have his own man. So "friends," interested and disinterested, were trying to

123

persuade Haig to leave for the sake of his President, his country and his reputation—the NATO appointment would not require Senate approval so he could beat the questions about his extraordinary White House tenure, and in ten years or so, write his memoirs.

Hartmann won the war of whispers, but he probably prevailed because, in the end, the President decided it had to be that way. What finally convinced Haig to leave was that Ford had approved a new White House organizational structure—just a piece of paper for the moment—that would place eight senior staff members at the same level as the chief of staff. Nine people would have open access to the Oval Office, the chief of staff's title would be changed to coordinator—it would end, at least for a while, the days when a Haig or a Haldeman could almost totally control the flow of information to a President.

The announcement came on September 16: Haig would leave the White House in two weeks to take over the NATO command. Five years earlier, Haig had been just another promising colonel in the Army, a colonel smart and lucky enough to get assigned to Henry Kissinger's staff. Now he was a four-star general, a very young one at 49, and he had served his country in ways only he knew. "Nothing on the battlefield," he said, "was as tough as this."

Haig had been in the White House seventeen months. Was he acting President part of that time? "I had to do things I would not have done under normal circumstances. You cannot avoid responsibility." Were there times, at the end, when President Nixon was irrational? "If there were, I wouldn't tell anybody . . . I am at peace with myself."

What a story Alexander Haig has to tell, if he ever chooses to. From sometime early in 1974 until September 30 of that year, under two Presidents, Haig had assumed on his own authority many of the principal functions of the leader of the most powerful nation on earth. The Presidency, the Oval Office, is a black box—crises and information go in, decisions and policy come out. The assumption and the faith is that the inner workings of the box are in the control of a President constitutionally selected in the name of 200 million Americans. But clearly that was not the case for most of 1974. In the disturbed Nixon White House and the chaotic Ford White House, no one but Haig himself knew how often he alone worked inside the box. "Al was running the place until the day he left," said a Ford man. "He must have looked around with stark terror. The White House was dissolving in his eyes and he couldn't let that happen. He is a West Point man; what does that motto mean to him? Duty. Honor. Country."

"I have several people in mind to replace General Haig," President Ford said. "I have made no decision yet." It was a harmless, if senseless, deception; the Rumsfeld decision was already made.

Rumsfeld's appointment as coordinator was announced eight days later. At 42, he was one of the youngest people around Ford. He had been elected a congressman from the wealthy Republican suburbs of Chicago at the age of 30, resigning his seat to serve Nixon as director of the Office of Economic Opportunity, director of the Cost of Living Council, counselor, and ambassador to NATO. By 1973, he was anxious to get back on the track toward high elected office; he sometimes said it was a mistake to give up his congressional seat.

"Rummy" does not make many mistakes. The first words that come to mind about him are "self-contained" or "controlled." He is short and muscular—he was captain of Princeton's wrestling team in 1954—and there is economy and coolness in his dress and movements. His conservative voting record was similar to Ford's when they were friends in Congress, and both had been Eagle Scouts, but Ford and Rumsfeld were not alike. It may be that the older man and the younger man represent two generations of Midwestern upward mobility, the Rotarian who throws his arm around your shoulder and the young man who glances at his watch as he

125

shakes hands. Rumsfeld had political talents Jerry Ford never wanted. Like John Kennedy or Richard Nixon, Rumsfeld could shed people without a tremor. There were other examples, but the best involved his long and now ended friendship with Allard Lowenstein, the evangelical young Democrat who had organized the "Dump Johnson" movement in 1968.

Rumsfeld and Lowenstein had been close friends since the late 1950's when both came to Washington as congressional aides. Their friendship transcended their very different politics —Rummy went to Democratic conventions with Al, and Al went to Republican conventions with Rummy. So it was only natural that Lowenstein, the president of Americans for Democratic Action, would come to his friend's defense in 1969, lobbying editors and Democratic congressmen when other liberals accused Rumsfeld of trying to destroy the Federal antipoverty program as Nixon's director of the Office of Economic Opportunity. And it was natural a year later, when Lowenstein was running for Congress, that Rumsfeld volunteered to defend him against Republican charges of advocating student violence.

What was not so natural was a flyer appearing two days later in which Rumsfeld endorsed Lowenstein's opponent under the headline "Lowenstein Debunked Again." The anti-Lowenstein brochures had obviously been prepared before Rumsfeld volunteered to speak out for his old friend, and Lowenstein was convinced that he had been set up for a Republican kill.

There were changes in the White House when Rumsfeld took over on October 1, and the staff reorganization allowed more people direct access to Ford. But sometimes there seemed to be more access than action, and one insider characterized the Ford-Rumsfeld style as "comfortable incompetence." Action memos were often replaced by long, rambling meetings with Ford calling people in from the hall outside the Oval Office and saying things like, "Rog, listen to this, what do you think about . . ." Or he would break into discussion with,

126

"That reminds me of the time . . ." and story-swapping would begin.

The tone was now Ford's, but at the level below the easy talk in the Oval Office and in the Cabinet and bureaus, the people and apparatus were still Nixon. There was little bureaucratic direction from the top; the problem was becoming both subversion of Ford policy and simulation in the absence of Ford policies.

Months after Rumsfeld took over, Charles Goodell came to Ford with a long list of explicit Presidential directives that had been ignored, changed or just lost by his subordinates. One of them involved a welfare regulation proposal from Caspar Weinberger, the holdover secretary of Health, Education and Welfare. The President objected to the proposal and ordered Weinberger to come back with "your best alternative." But after two months, and after Ford had forgotten the whole thing, there was no alternative from Weinberger. In fact, the secretary and other Nixon holdovers in the Office of Management and Budget were quietly implementing the regulations which Ford had specifically disapproved.

Goodell was not the only old Ford friend who was frustrated, even slightly frantic, about his reluctance or inability to put his own stamp on the Presidency. Barber Conable, his old colleague in the Republican House leadership, wrote Ford a long letter that ended: "You are letting the old apparatus define the character and goals of your administration . . . You should control the staff rather than letting the staff control you."

But Conable was probably wrong in his analysis. Ford, on his own terms, was in control. He was the President. He loved the job—as he loved to say—and the character of the administration was his own character, which the press and nation seemed to find splendid. Goals? He had no goals—Ford was a product of a system where the goal was win the job. He had won it. He was the President.

In a way it was worse than the movie *The Candidate*, where

127

Robert Redford is elected a U.S. senator and then pulls his campaign manager into an empty room to ask, "What do we do now?" Ford did not have to wait for an election night or votes to be counted. He had been pretty sure months before August 9 that he was going to be President. And he had done nothing to prepare himself for actually doing the job; all his efforts and advice, mainly from Bob Hartmann, were aimed at getting the job.

Ford never wondered what to do next. There was never a review of Nixon policy, before or after his own inaugural. He simply accommodated himself to the situation as he found it, initialing the action memos as they came by, listening to Kissinger, placing friends around him, having his picture taken and, in his own words, "loving every minute of it."

AFTER Haig's departure was announced, according to Ron Nessen, "Poor Al just wandered around here for a week—he didn't know what to do with himself."

Nessen's deliberately snide comment could be interpreted as a backhanded tribute to the control Haig had exercised. In that week, the public got a glimpse of the casual and slightly unhinged workings of the Ford White House. The President said his Central Intelligence Agency had the right to decide what was best for people in other countries, nominated a man pejoratively nicknamed "Mr. Fixit" for allegedly selling U.S. ambassadorships as (what else?) an ambassador, and came damn close to threatening a nuclear war over oil. To round things out, the chairman of the President's Council of Economic Advisers offered the opinion that the Americans being hurt most by the sagging economy were stockbrokers on Wall Street—an opinion that was loudly jeered by his audience of labor leaders.

And that was not quite all. Ford announced his Vietnam amnesty plan on September 16, and it was harsher than some people had expected, or, perhaps, it was just harsher than the treatment of Nixon a week earlier. There was not, it seemed, to be equal justice under the law for former Presidents and

129

draft resisters. But there was a consistency revealed in the nature of Gerald Ford: the generosity and consideration he had always shown individuals rarely was extended to people in the abstract. He would, someone had said years before, give his lunch to a hungry child, then vote against a free milk program for poor schoolchildren.

There was also a consistency in the sloppy staff work in the White House. Someone had screwed things up between the Oval Office, the Defense Department and the Justice Department, and the amnesty plan had a loophole no one in authority had noticed—principled draft evaders might have to serve two years in punitive public service jobs to regain their rights of citizenship, but deserters only had to take an oath of allegiance to the United States.*

Amnesty, however, was forgotten for the moment when Ford held his second news conference that night and was asked, as he knew he would be, about reports that the CIA had spent at least $8 million in Chile in covert opposition to the elected government of a Marxist, Salvador Allende, between 1970 and Allende's assassination in 1973. Whatever else he was, Ford was brutally candid: "I am not going to pass judgment on whether it is permitted or authorized under international law . . . I think this is in the best interest of the people of Chile, and certainly in our best interest."

One reporter asked if the Soviet Union had the right to choose what was best for other countries, say, Canada. The President would not comment, but the world had a lot to say the next day about American morality and/or stupidity. The *Times* in London talked about morality, offering the opinion that Ford had ended the illusions of anyone who thought American international conduct was "sometimes clumsy, often misunderstood, but fundamentally honorable."

---

* Only about 22,500 of the 126,900 young Americans eligible for conditional amnesty applied to the government before the program was terminated six months later. The rest chose to remain outside the country or as official fugitives from justice.

130

If the President had the right to decide what is best for the people of Chile, he certainly had the right to nominate an ambassador to Spain—and Kissinger and Haig had combined to persuade him to nominate Peter Flanigan, executive director of the Council on International Economic Policy under Nixon.

The nomination was incredible. Flanigan—the "Mr. Fixit" of the Nixon White House—was not charged with any Watergate crime, but Herbert Kalmbach, Nixon's former personal attorney, had testified under oath to the House Judiciary Committee's impeachment inquiry that Flanigan brokered ambassadorships in return for massive contributions to the 1972 Nixon campaign: "Peter said, 'Herb, we would like you to contact a Dr. Ruth Farkas in New York. She is interested in giving $250,000 for Costa Rica.' " Mrs. Farkas, according to Kalmbach, thought Costa Rica was not worth that much, but she and her husband did contribute $300,000, and she was appointed ambassador to Luxembourg.

The Senate Foreign Relations Committee just tabled the nomination, but Ford refused to withdraw it, even while his staff was leaking stories that the nomination was really only some kind of high-level clerical error. The day it was tabled, Patrick Buchanan, Nixon-Agnew's toughest speech writer, decided to resign from the White House staff. Kissinger and Haig had promised Buchanan he would become U.S. Ambassador to South Africa. Ford was willing to make the nomination, but obviously the Senate wasn't about to confirm Nixon's last loyalists as America's representatives around the world.

The next day it was announced that consumer prices were rising nationally at 1.3 per cent a month. Questioned about that, Alan Greenspan, chairman of the President's Council of Economic Advisers, said, "If you really want to examine, percentagewise, who was hurt most in their income, it was Wall Street brokers." Percentagewise he was quite accurate, just as it would have been accurate to say that amountwise Nelson Rockefeller was hurt most because his personal portfolio had dropped $30 million in value as the stock market declined.

131

But it was an asinine, insensitive accuracy, especially because Greenspan chose to offer it at a meeting of labor leaders whose union members were earning a lot less than even depressed brokers.

The President then traveled to the United Nations on September 18 and warned, in not too veiled tones, that if the Arabs could use their oil and prices as political weapons, we could use our resources in the same way, and he reminded delegates that many of their countries needed our most abundant resource, food.

If the President of the United States then seemed to be on record as saying he would let people starve to lower American gasoline prices, he went a lot further on September 23, when he told a World Energy Conference in Detroit: "Throughout history, nations have gone to war over natural advantages such as water, or food . . . It is difficult to discuss the energy problem without lapsing into doomsday language. The danger is clear. It is severe."

The reaction was severe, too. Arab headlines screamed of imminent war, European editorials questioned American sanity, and American diplomats were beseiged by calls and visits from foreign counterparts wanting to know if it was true, if the United States was considering war. It wasn't true and Ford, among some of his staff, seemed genuinely surprised by the uproar.

Hell, he had been calling for war and escalation of wars for twenty-five years! He had also been calling for UFO investigations and impeachment of Supreme Court justices, but no one paid that much attention. He was talking like a congressman, but the world was listening to a President. As Charlie Goodell had predicted, Jerry Ford was slow in making the transition from congressman to national leader. He was still of a world where if a member says something too silly or scary on the floor of the House, he can have the text changed in the next day's Congressional Record—that privilege has always been a blessing to the drunks in Congress whose re-

132

marks sometimes have to be rewritten to make any sense at all.

The new President also had not grasped the difference between rhetoric to score political points and policy to effect political change; a congressman is much more comfortable with the former. The doomsday rhetoric was written by Secretary of State Kissinger—Kissinger was warning of "nuclear catastrophe" at the same time—to convince other oil-producing nations that the United States would not stand still for continually escalating world petroleum prices.

But, in fact, the United States, Ford and Kissinger, had no policy or plan to do anything about oil prices. There was no fuel conservation at home, and each month the United States was importing more foreign oil than the month before. We were helping build the sellers' market.

"The basic problem is that Ford does not really believe there is a long-term energy crisis," Federal Energy Administrator John Sawhill said privately at the time of the war talk. "He has not grasped production and consumption figures and projections. He only understands long lines at gas stations. We have no policy. It was mainly Kissinger's frustration. He had expected that because of his efforts in the Middle East and his friends, the Saudis, that oil prices would come down. But they didn't, so he's angry."

Kissinger's anger was American foreign policy. The secretary, as far as anyone at the White House could tell, had absolute control over foreign affairs. "Take that up with Dr. Kissinger" was Ford's standard line when foreign policy came up in the Oval Office. When Ford and French President Giscard d'Estaing were planning later for their first summit on the Caribbean island of Martinique, the French asked several times for private meetings between the presidents—really private with no foreign ministers and photographers. No, answered the State Department, Kissinger must be present. It got to the point that the French press and officials began referring to Gerald Ford as "the man who is accompanying Henry Kissinger to Martinique."

WASHINGTON is not a nice place. The glamorous part of the city, the white enclave almost surrounded by almost unseen blacks, has one overriding business, politics, and politics is not a nice business. It is a dangerous business for amateurs, and John Sawhill, the Federal Energy administrator, was an amateur. He thought he was in the government business or the energy crisis business and when he finally realized he was in politics, it was too late—he was in no business. Jerry Ford fired him.

Sawhill took his job and himself very seriously. He was promoted from assistant administrator to administrator three months before Ford became President, and he had used his time in the agency well, studying small mountains of data on American energy production and consumption, picking the brains of the economists, engineers and managers inside and outside the oil industry. His basic conclusion was simple enough: The United States had no choice except to reduce fuel consumption because domestic production could never meet existing American demand, and the cost of foreign oil would inevitably remain too high to be absorbed indefinitely within a stable economic structure.

But in fact, American consumption of foreign oil had

steadily risen since the Arab oil embargo of early 1973 and seven million barrels of oil were coming into American ports each day at an annual cost of $24 billion, compared with $2.7 billion worth of imports just four years earlier. The United States, Sawhill believed, could not continue to depend on Henry Kissinger's conviction that by himself he could cajole or bully the oil producers to stabilize world prices. The energy chief was sure Kissinger was wrong and believed the President would understand that as soon as he had all the facts.

Playing politics with nothing but facts was heady stuff, headier than Sawhill knew. He had spent most of his life as a professor, economist and credit management executive before joining the Office of Management and Budget and then shifting over to FEA. He knew very little about political men; he did not know that facts and reasonable arguments are not the coin of their realm. Politicians deal with the shadows of facts, the imprecise perceptions of reality projected in public and accepted by the public. Politicians do not survive by knowing what is true, but by knowing and shaping what is believed to be true. And although government is not strictly politics, government is largely politicians.

In ways Sawhill did not understand, his fact-packed memos to the President never seemed to get all the way into the Oval Office. So he decided to go public and persuade the leader of this new open administration. He started by accepting an invitation to appear on the "Today" show of October 1. Bill Monroe, the show's Washington editor, asked him what should be done about the energy crisis and Sawhill told him: put a 20-cents-a-gallon tax on gasoline to cut consumption.

Until the United States made a serious effort to cut its fuel consumption, Sawhill reasoned, it would not have leverage or credibility to bargain for world price stabilization. As long as we continued to pay any price asked, why should the Arabs take Presidential threats seriously, even threats of food embargoes and invasion?

That made headlines. Sawhill quickly found out how seductive it is to see your own name in 36-point type. Energy was a

136

big story and Sawhill liked reporters. Once he even let John Bishop of *Newsweek* listen on an extension phone while the president of an oil company tried to get him to fire one of his assistants at FEA. At the White House, Ford asserted again that there would never be a gas tax as long as he was President, but Ron Nessen said Sawhill could speak his mind: "This is an open administration, and people are free to say what they want."

Sawhill was not alone in believing a gas tax was necessary. Other advisers told Ford the same thing—William Simon, who had preceded Sawhill in the energy job, Interior Secretary Rogers Morton, who had just been named the administration's chief energy spokesman, and William Seidman, among others—but Ford would not be moved. He said privately that he remembered the unpopularity of World War II gasoline taxes and that a 1974 tax would haunt the Republican party and defeat its candidates for years. Any tax, he said, would be "over my dead body." Simon, Morton and Seidman heard the President's mind clang shut and had the political sense to keep quiet.

Sawhill kept at it. He is a very direct man. When he was asked about energy policy at a closed Senate hearing, he said, "The administration does not have a policy or set of policies directed at halting and reversing the rise in world oil prices in the short run." Henry Kissinger heard about that within hours and went into a small rage. Who was this John Sawhill?

Simon and Morton were already his enemies, although Sawhill did not seem to know it. Simon had resented Sawhill for not deferring to his lead and advice when he moved up from Simon's assistant to administrator. Morton, who had served in Congress with Ford and was supposed to be the President's energy spokesman, had nothing to say because Ford had nothing to say, and he was unhappy at being ignored by the press. Sawhill had plenty to say and data to back it up, so reporters gathered around his desk.

Without knowing it, Sawhill was on one of Washington's beaten paths to oblivion. Subordinates defer to men with the ear of the President; Kissinger, Simon and Morton were all Oval Office regulars—and they weren't in there to praise the candor or build the career of John Sawhill. There were no rising media stars in the Ford administration—Kissinger and Simon were press favorites before August 9—and Ford's people were very careful not to openly upstage the boss. He was the one with a round-the-clock photographer.

On October 17, Sawhill got a call from John Bishop, his friend on *Newsweek,* saying the magazine had a tip he was going to be pushed out—what did he have to say about that? He had nothing to say, he was stunned. Nobody had said anything to him.

Sawhill started checking around. Morton told him, "John, the President has problems with you." Friends in Congress— Sawhill had made a lot of them in his six months on the job, most of them the wrong ones, liberal Democrats—told him some of his problems were with a group of tough senators who thought the oil companies were basically none of the government's business and were upset about Sawhill's warnings that the industry should do nothing to encourage retail gasoline sales.

The senators—Paul Fannin and Barry Goldwater of Arizona, James McClure of Idaho, Dewey Bartlett of Oklahoma and Clifford Hansen of Wyoming—were all fairly close to Ford, and they had sent him a message from the oil companies: dump Sawhill. It is part of Sawhill's charm and naïveté that he never made the connection between telling an oil company president to go to hell—with a reporter listening on an extension—and the subsequent pressure by five western senators who wanted his head on a platter. He was working for a President whose best friends were important business lobbyists and who actually planned to become one of them until fate and Watergate intervened.

On October 21, *Newsweek* predicted Sawhill's demise, and the administrator decided to talk to the President himself. He caught Ford between trips, on October 25.

138

It was an uncomfortable meeting, as Sawhill remembered it, because Ford really did not like to fire people.

"I can't function this way," said Sawhill, who exaggerated a bit. "I'm spending half my day talking to reporters asking if I'm going to keep my job."

"I like you, John, I like you very much," Ford said. "I'd like you to stay."

Sawhill said he felt very deeply that the country needed an energy conservation program, a strong one. "I don't think voluntary measures is a program," he went on. "I'm willing to resign, Mr. President."

They talked for a while more, but Ford finally said, "Well, maybe it would be better . . . Would you like to stay in government? I'll find you a first-rate job, a good, high-level job."

"I had the distinct feeling," Sawhill said later, "that he would have been happy, that I could have kept the job, if I just said I could find some way to accommodate myself to what was going on." The resignation was announced four days later in an exchange of letters in which Sawhill again plugged for energy conservation, and Ford renewed the new job pledge. Sawhill was later offered an appointment to an obscure Defense Department board that renegotiates military contracts if economic conditions change.

Ford announced a new FEA chief the same day. He was in a hurry because Congress and the press were getting on his back about the obvious lack of any energy policy that went beyond urging people to wear sweaters. In politics, when talk wears thin, you appoint. Ford appointed a "new team that will be in charge of the energy program, which we will see moving ahead, I think, under the stewardship of Rog Morton." The new team had old faces except for Sawhill's replacement, Andrew Gibson, a Rumsfeld friend and former Federal Maritime administrator. Gibson was president of Interstate Oil Transport, Inc., of Philadelphia.

Gibson was a disaster. He had worked for Interstate, which

139

was half-owned by Cities Service Oil, for less than a year and had a separation agreement with the company that would pay him $88,000 a year for the next ten years. It also turned out that as chairman of the Maritime Subsidy Board, Gibson had approved a complicated subsidy arrangement under which the Federal government would pay a $90.6 million subsidy for the construction of three oil tankers that would be chartered for twenty years to a subsidiary of Interstate.

Ron Nessen said that the White House had been unaware of the arrangement, and Ford intended to go ahead with the nomination of Gibson. The nominee contradicted that, saying that he had explained the $88,000-a-year deal to William Walker, a former Rumsfeld aide at OEO, who was handling personnel at the White House, and Walker told him, "Don't worry about it."

The White House later amended its version to say that someone was aware of a separation agreement between Gibson and the company but was unaware of the circumstances and amount.

The White House and Andrew Gibson held out for thirteen days, but on November 11 Gibson requested that the President not submit his nomination to the Senate, and Ford replied that he would "reluctantly" agree. Two days later Rogers Morton, like Sawhill before him, said a gasoline tax might be necessary to reduce American oil consumption. The President was in Phoenix, Arizona, for a press conference, and when the question came up, he answered: "I don't know how many times I have to say that we are not considering an additional gas tax . . . I thought that others in the executive branch got the word, and I hope this word is conveyed to my good friend the secretary of the Interior."

So Sawhill, staying on the payroll as a consultant, was in charge of FEA until the end of the year. This time, though, he kept his mouth shut. He had learned something about Washington. Take away the big titles, the big names, the big numbers and the big headlines, and what do you have? Office politics.

140

"I was very naïve," Sawhill said after it was over and he was leaving town to become president of New York University. "I believed Nessen that day when he said it was an open administration."

5

The Leader

"If Lincoln were alive today, he'd roll over in his grave."

House Minority Leader Ford,
at a Lincoln Day dinner

ERALD FORD could never quite get over the fact that *he* made Nelson Rockefeller Vice-President of the United States. When he was asked at a press conference on November 14 to list the achievements of his first hundred days as President, Ford said, "Number one, nominating Nelson Rockefeller."

Number one achievement? He had to nominate someone and Rockefeller seemed the logical choice. Well, he handled the question better than his friend William Scott, a senator from Virginia since 1973. When Scott was asked, early in 1974, what had been "the highlight" of his first year in the Senate, he answered, after a moment of thought, "Being sworn in."

In private, Ford was as fascinated as any other upwardly mobile American with the details of Rockefeller wealth that came out in the confirmation hearings after the appointment on August 20. "Can you imagine, Dave," he said to his friend and photographer, David Kennerly, after reading the *Post* and the *Times* one morning, "Nelson *lost* $30 million in one year and it didn't make any difference."

Just about the only thing that made any difference to Nelson Rockefeller any more was becoming President. He had resigned after fifteen years as governor of New York in late 1973 to begin his fourth run for the Republican nomination for President. When Nixon resigned, Rockefeller's only title was chairman of the family-financed Commission on Critical Choices for America—Ford was a member—and he was using the commission as a base, traveling the country trying to convince Republican groups that he was one of them, that his suspect New York liberalism had mellowed into solid Republican conformity. His party did not fully believe that, and his running sometimes looked liked crawling. He went to Southern Republican conferences to tell the same people who had brutally jeered him out of the 1964 GOP Convention for opposing Barry Goldwater that they had been right all along: "I don't think the ideological differences were as important as they seemed then, or as some of us made them out to be."

Rockefeller was beyond ideology, beyond arrogance, beyond cynicism. Hypermetabolic and hyperbolic by nature, he was capable of saying anything, once stopping a mind-boggling defense of Nixon's integrity to look up at an audience of Midwestern Republicans and shout: "Let's hear it for the Founding Fathers. I think they did a hell of a job!" During his confirmation hearings, he threw out lines like, "Things like this hurt the average taxpayer like you and me," and, "I have a place in Westchester"—the place was Pocantico Hills, six square miles of the most pampered and most valuable real estate on the planet.

He was still "Rocky" on the streets—he was called "Mr. Nelson" in the hushed New York offices of the family—and he was probably the best campaigner in America. He most likely would have been President if he could have won a Republican nomination in the 1960's, but that never happened because, unlike Gerald Ford, he was an alien in the party. More than anything else, the Republican party is the institutionalization of America's small towns and corporate ethic, and Republicans never really trusted him; he was too cosmopolitan, too securely rich, too *New York*. "The biggest

148

mistake I ever made was not becoming a Democrat," he once told a friend. "You can buy the Democratic nomination—the Kennedys did. You can't buy Republicans, they really believe it."

President Ford, this time, stepped outside the limits of his past—Rockefeller was not the cautious choice. Ford had made the decision alone—the discussions with friends were essentially information-gathering. The President was not afraid that Rockefeller would "dominate the administration"—a ridiculous concern of some of his friends who did not understand the realities of any President-Vice-President relationship—and he was confident that he could handle the conservatives in the party who would forever despise Rockefeller.

It was Jerry Ford at his best, decisive and in balance with himself and the world. The only other Republican he seriously considered was Republican National Chairman George Bush, a safer choice, a friend from Congress, a comfortable man not that different from Ford himself. Ford and Rockefeller were not really friends, but the President wanted a Vice-President who would bring stature and a national constituency to an administration short on both. Ford had always believed in the balanced ticket; he had privately recommended John Lindsay as Richard Nixon's running mate in 1968. "It's perfect," said one enthusiastic Washington Republican, "Rocky's from the East, Ford's from the Midwest; Rocky's liberal, Ford is conservative; Rocky's capable, Ford's . . ." He didn't finish the sentence, pausing for an embarrassed moment and saying, "Well, it would make a damn good ticket in '76."

Rockefeller was indeed capable, even if his competence was sometimes frightening. In New York, he had made the Republican party and important segments of the Democratic party into extensions of his person and money; he had built a major state university system where before nothing existed; and he had taken about a third of state government and shifted it from public to personal control. One measure of Rockefeller's competence and power could be calculated stat-

149

istically: when he took office in 1959, more than 90 per cent of New York's governmental expenditures were accounted for in the state budget; when he left, only about 60 per cent were detailed for public view.

What Rockefeller had done, in the simplest terms and in the name of efficiency, was to break off parts and functions of government and set them up as quasi-public, semiautonomous units—the Metropolitan Transportation Authority, the Urban Development Corporation—and then selected the boards governing the units. To ensure absolute personal control, he chose the chief executives of the authorities and corporations and literally bought them, paid for them in cash. During his Vice-Presidential confirmation hearings, scrutiny of his tax returns revealed that he had given cash gifts in the hundreds of thousands of dollars to authority directors and his personal staff, including Henry Kissinger, who was his foreign policy adviser until 1969. Even with governors like Franklin Roosevelt and Thomas Dewey, New York had never had a foreign policy until Rockefeller came along.

The workings of the Rockefeller mind are a wonder to behold. After he became Vice-President, Rockefeller told a questioner that he never spoke out against U.S. involvement in Vietnam because he did not want to offend Presidents Johnson and Nixon and risk reductions in Federal aid to his state. "I can see you never ran for public office," he said to the questioner. "I was elected governor of New York and my responsibility was to the people of New York. You don't kick people in Washington in the shins if you expect them to do something for you."

That is not quite what he had told me privately in June 1970, soon after President Nixon had ordered the invasion of Cambodia. Rockefeller said then that he was afraid to speak out because of Nixon's emotional condition. He said he did not want to be the one to push Nixon too far, that there was no telling what the man might do. "It is a very dangerous situation," he said. Rockefeller was telling me that

150

he thought the President of the United States was nuts. I knew his source was Kissinger, but I could not bring myself to believe what I heard—that was my mistake. It was another mistake to underrate how far beyond cynicism politicians are capable of going. When Rockefeller began campaigning like a dervish for Nixon in 1972, I naïvely took that as some kind of proof that he had been talking without thinking in our conversation two summers earlier.

In that same conversation, Rockefeller told me that if he were President he would not resist the Cooper-Church Amendment and other congressional attempts to end the war. I asked why, knowing that he believed in the American involvement. *Look,* he said, and I am paraphrasing his words, *we've lost the war and we have to get out. When we do, the Communists are going to take over South Vietnam and a couple of other countries and when that happens there'll be hell to pay at home. The people are going to have to blame someone. Why not let Congress take the blame? Let the history books say you were forced to give up by the Congress. I can't understand why Dick doesn't realize that.*

Rockefeller, however, did not have any significant impact inside the early Ford White House—he was too busy trying to get himself confirmed. The Senate and House hearings dragged on for four months.

When the President and his nominee were together, Rockefeller was almost obsequious, restraining his normally ebullient conversation and punctuating it incessantly with, "Yes, Mr. President."

ERALD FORD did not assume the Presidency in ordinary times. Consumer prices were rising at a compound rate of 16.8 per cent, unemployment was at 5.3 per cent, the Gross National Product was dropping at an annual rate of 4.2 per cent, home-building had practically stopped as mortgages were carrying interest rates as high as 10.5 per cent, and the Dow-Jones Industrial average on the New York Stock Exchange dropped ninety-nine points in his first month in office and another fifty points in the week after he pardoned Nixon, the worst month-long slump since the great crash of 1929.

Inflation was "Public Enemy Number One," the new President had told Congress in his first address to a joint session on August 12. He offered no answers for the debilitating combination of inflation and recession that gripped the country —no one else seemed sure what to do either—but he bought time and *showed that he cared* by endorsing a month-old Senate resolution calling for a "Domestic Summit Meeting" of public officials, economists, businessmen, labor leaders and other concerned Americans to consider the national illness. It was a classic act of creative caution, but a widely praised one. Public attention would be called to the depths of the

153

problems and perhaps to the need for real change in the American life style. Besides, the new President was the first to admit he did not know much about economics—*"No politicians know anything about economics,"* said Barber Conable—and this was one way to start learning.

The basic economic views of Gerald Ford had been molded by the kind of men who waited for him back home in Alexandria. There was a party at his house after the joint address, and the people there were his closest friends and advisers— William Whyte of U.S. Steel; Bryce Harlow of Procter & Gamble; Rodney Markley, chief Washington lobbyist of the Ford Motor Company; William Seidman, head of a multi-million-dollar accounting firm with headquarters in Grand Rapids; and a trio of Ford's conservative buddies from the old days in the House, Mel Laird, John Marsh and John Byrnes. Whyte walked around Ford's living room telling anyone who would listen that the answer to the country's economic troubles was "more profits."

"More profits" has traditionally been the cornerstone of the Republican economic credo. Most politicians in the Grand Old Party really do believe in free enterprise, less government interference and, deep in their hearts, that what is good for General Motors is good for the country. Of course, they cannot always say those things in public, but that they blame on the public, which they see as too simple-minded to understand what Calvin Coolidge told them—business is the business of America. Before he decided to bug his own office, President Nixon told two of his assistants that he thought 8 per cent unemployment would be good for the country— a little suffering is good for people, to toughen them up, make them appreciate what they have, cut the damn unions down to size, stop this inflation. That's the old-time Republican religion and it's where Ford began: tight money, business incentives, reduced government expenditures for everything but defense and, when necessary, a little double talk for the simple-minded.

154

As it happened, on the day Ford took office, General Motors announced that it was raising its automobile and truck prices by 10 per cent, about $500 a unit. There was no White House reaction until after a day of badgering at the doors of the press office. Finally the new President issued a statement saying he was "disappointed" and hoped other auto companies would not follow the GM lead—which, of course, they immediately did, raising their prices an average of 8 per cent.

After two weeks of telephone calls from Nixon's old economic counselor, Kenneth Rush, a former president of Union Carbide, GM announced a price reduction of $54 a unit. Ford said he was "delighted"—at 10 per cent he was disappointed, but at 9 per cent he was delighted.*

On September 5, as part of the build-up for the Economic Summit, the President sat down in the East Room for a meeting—a one-student seminar, really—with a dozen stars of the economics departments of American universities. It was a balanced group of brilliant, egocentric and often wrong scholars and sometime policymakers ranging, left to right, from John Kenneth Galbraith of Harvard to Milton Friedman of the University of Chicago. The President listened for hours, but he heard only what he wanted to hear. What he never heard, however, was a forecast of how bad things were actually going to get, that within a few months American unemployment would be soaring toward 10 per cent.

Alan Greenspan, his house economist, opened the session by predicting no slump in capital output. The summation of the eight hours of talk was made by Arthur Okun of the Brookings Institution, who once held Greenspan's job as chairman of the Council of Economic Advisers. There was

* Rush became something of a symbol of the confusion in the early Ford White House. On August 29, he was introduced with some fanfare as chairman of the revived Cost of Living Council and the administration's chief economic spokesman. Six days later, on September 4, he was named ambassador to France.

no consensus, he said, but there was a direction—down: "A flat to a slightly falling Gross National Product for nine months or so . . . rising unemployment [and] some modest improvement in inflation . . . Within the range of the possible amounts of Federal spending that we will have, the lower the figure, the slightly better news will be on inflation and the slightly worse news will be on unemployment, but that there is not a qualitatively great difference there . . . A few people mentioned that it might be counterproductive to make commitments to budget balance in a weakening economy."

At the end of the day, a White House wit who was there bet a reporter five inflated dollars that Ford would go the other way, insisting on a balanced budget, spending cuts and a tax increase. "You know who's coming over for dinner tonight?" he said. "Herbert Hoover."

The Conference on Inflation, as the economic summit was officially known, was called in Washington on September 27 and 28. Eight hundred Americans were named as delegates, and on the evening before the conference, air traffic in and out of Washington's National Airport was delayed up to two hours as one hundred private jets landed, bringing in their single important passengers to talk about inflation, recession and energy conservation.

The conference was hardly a compelling spectacle—within a couple of hours three-quarters of the delegate chairs were empty—but it revealed a great deal about the United States and its leaders. The President found his comfort in clichés, turning on the Muzak of American politics: "I have unlimited confidence in America," etc., etc., etc. Congressional leaders, however, were secure in their role, the role Ford himself was conditioned for. Carl Albert, the Speaker of the House, began by saying, "Congressional input has been limited in conference planning". . . The Speaker pointed his little finger at the White House, emphasizing that Congress *cared* but—God forbid!—it was not *responsible* for anything past, present or future. Albert and other congressional types presented them-

156

selves as concerned observers and critics—I wondered why they just didn't go ahead and ask for press credentials.

The delegates, despite rhetoric about "the people" and "the American spirit," were a collection of special interests. Labor leaders led by George Meany, president of the AFL-CIO, argued against wage controls and proposed money-moving antirecession programs. Farm organization leaders argued against restrictive export regulations designed to keep more American food at home and reduce food prices. Business leaders called for greater depreciation allowances to increase industrial production. Oil executives wanted an end to price controls on domestic petroleum production. Airline executives wanted more fuel price controls. Henry Ford II wanted a five-year moratorium on installation of pollution-control and safety devices on his cars. State and local officials wanted to preserve public service spending and cut defense spending. "Spokesmen" for the poor attacked defense spending, depreciation allowances and business tax credits, advocating more social programs.

On that level, the summit and the ten mini-summits that preceded it were a useful exercise in demonstrating that James Madison was right in believing that "countervailing forces" would keep the United States free. The idea he presented 200 years ago was that we were a nation of conflicting groups and special interests that would thrash out differences in the arena of Congress. The President, in addition to overseeing the implementation of law by the executive branch, would be the embodiment of a united nation. He would be the leader.

Coming from Congress, Gerald Ford had no real conception of what leadership was. Now he was earnestly trying to develop a concept in his own mind. The trouble he was having doing that was revealed again in his words to the summit delegates: "In this battle there is no substitute for candor and hard work."

Candor and hard work had become the rhetoric and the

157

reality of Ford's young Presidency. He rarely spoke without using the words "candid" and "open" about himself and his White House. But words did not make it so.

A candid assessment of the summit, if the President had wanted to offer one, was that it was a media event calculated to impress the country that its leader was doing something about their economic problems. I would estimate, as a willing co-conspirator during ten years as a political reporter, that American politicians and Presidents spend half their working hours planning and participating in events staged specifically for newspapers and television, noncommittal events that only show the performing politician is aware a problem exists and is busy—walking through slums or factories, visiting Vietnam and welcoming planeloads of wounded soldiers or war orphans. Obviously, symbolic gestures are part of governing and leadership, but as television cameras roam the land the symbolism is coming dangerously close to being the substance.

The other half of Ford's battle plan, hard work, was the subject of constant bulletins from his White House—the President was in the office by 7 A.M., he has traveled "x" thousands of miles, his favorite homily was "Eating and sleeping are a waste of time." He was something of a human media event himself, he seemed satisfied as long as he was moving. Work, to him, was an end rather than a means. The long hours and sweaty walks through Harlem show that politicians care but in the end they are no substitute for policy or leadership— it just looks like leadership on television.

When the economic conference ended with another roaring jam of private jets at National Airport, Ford and his money men went back to the White House to do the real work of making nothing, or at least no change, look like something. Ford had the same economic advisers as Nixon—Greenspan, Simon and Ash—and they had no intention of abandoning their own policies. They were actively fostering a contained recession by encouraging policies like tight money, believing

158

that a mild slump would curb inflation in a few months. "All of Ford's policies provide the appearance of action which can at best be only marginal in economic effect," said one of his advisers, candidly but off the record, after the Ford programs were announced. "But if they buy us time and let us pursue the basic work of belt-tightening, then they are probably worth it."

Of course, the President was not about to go on television and tell the American people, particularly the 6 per cent who were then unemployed and millions more who thought they might be next, that a little recession would be good for them in the long run. So Bill Seidman and Milton Friedman, a veteran Ford speech writer with the same name as the economist, tried to make it sound quite the opposite in the first draft of the speech Ford was scheduled to deliver to a joint session of Congress on October 8.

On Monday, October 7, after the draft had been turned over to Bob Hartmann for polishing, the President called Simon, Ash and Seidman into his office: "I want to compliment you on a good job. I challenge anyone to do a better job."

"A disaster!" pronounced Hartmann, and once he got his hands on the draft, no one else saw it again until minutes before Ford began reading the words at a televised joint session of the Congress. Hiding, bluffing and fuming, Hartmann kept Simon and Ash from learning what he was doing. He saw his job as politics and had a strong sense that Republican economics sounds better in board rooms than at campaign stops. The President's reading copy was still being typed thirty minutes before he spoke; by then Hartmann had eliminated, among other things, proposals to drastically weaken national clean air standards to allow more use of coal.

Hartmann and Ford also got some help from Benton & Bowles, the New York advertising agency. The White House wanted a slogan for a volunteer campaign to do something

159

about the nation's economic problems. The admen came up with "Whip Inflation Now." Get it? WIN!*

Volunteerism. The last refuge of creative caution. You can do it! If Theodore Roosevelt saw being President as being the man in the arena, Gerald Ford was going to be the man in the bleachers, the cheerleader urging the nation to win this one for the Big $. Ford admired Harry Truman, but unfortunately he had reversed the roles of leader and country —instead of the country yelling "Give 'em Hell, Jerry!", he was yelling "Give 'em Hell, America!" Their President was behind them all the way.

With the first WIN button on his lapel, the President greeted Congress on October 8 with bows to the past and leadership: "In his first inaugural address, President Franklin D. Roosevelt said, and I quote: 'The people of the United States have not failed . . . they want direct, vigorous action, and they have asked for discipline and direction under our leadership.' . . . We must whip inflation right now."

The actual Ford proposal was neutral, deliberately counterbalancing in the effect it would have on the economy. The crux of the program was a one-year 5 per cent surcharge on the income taxes of corporations and the upper 28 per cent of individual taxpayers that would raise a projected $3 billion.

* Sylvia Porter, who writes an advice-to-consumers column for 346 newspapers, was the mother of the WIN program. At a financial mini-summit conference on September 20, she was allotted three minutes to speak and said: "There is an unspoken cry in the hearts of millions of us—'What can I do?'—that the President can and should answer . . . All consumer groups covering all types of organizations, educational, religious, civic, whatever, should be invited. The help of professionals in the fields of public relations, advertising, and the like, should be enlisted . . . The President himself should issue a major policy statement and kick off the call for voluntary action cooperation via a prime-time TV address . . . Victory gardens . . . Recycling . . . Energy conservation . . . As the Red Cross teaches swimming, so it could teach other vital subjects . . . It could easily be carried on from here and have an electrifying effect." Ford loved it and adopted it almost word for word, making Ms. Porter chairman of a Citizens' Action Committee to Fight Inflation.

That $3 billion would be redistributed in increased unemployment benefits and public service jobs in depressed areas and an increase in business investment tax credits from 7 to 10 per cent. The rest was "pledging" (a reduction in the current budget to the magic $300 billion, unspecified programs to reduce domestic oil consumption by one million barrels a day), "appointing" (Rogers Morton to head a new National Energy Board to figure out how to save those one million barrels), and "WINning."

"One week from tonight I have a long-standing invitation in Kansas City to address the Future Farmers of America, a fine organization of wonderful young people whose help, with millions of others, is vital in this battle. I will elaborate then how inflation fighters and energy savers can further mobilize their total efforts . . . The symbol of this new mobilization, the button which I am wearing on my lapel, bears the single word WIN."

On to Kansas City. The big WIN speech did not seem big enough to the three television networks. CBS, NBC and ABC informed the White House that they would not require live television facilities at the Municipal Auditorium—not enough news value, television said after hearing what Ford planned to do. Televise or else was the message back from Ron Nessen to his old bosses at NBC and their counterparts at the other networks. A very angry press secretary, in the President's name, the name of the man who appoints the Federal Communications Commission which regulates television, formally requested a suspension of regular programming for a live nationwide telecast. It took the networks about a half-hour to agree.

It may not have been news, but it certainly was entertaining. The President of the United States was reading his mail and telling people, as he had been told as a boy, to clean off their plates.

"America is arousing itself, as it always does in time of great challenge, to prove that we are a people who can do anything we want to do when we really want to do it," he told 13,000 future farmers. "We are going to win in America."

Then he began to run through winning recommendations from citizens and his new Citizens' Action Committee to Fight Inflation:

"Robert Stewart writes from Waverly, Tennessee, that he has a heart condition, unfortunately, and draws a pension of only $251.28 a month. This allows him just two meals a day. 'But thank God, we are not on welfare,' says Mr. Stewart. He asks me, and again I quote, 'Cut our government spending except for national defense.'

"Mr. Tennant is a self-taught machinist and a veteran who lost his leg in Korea. But it is his ability rather than his disability that comes through in his dear wife's letter. The Tennants write that they do not use credit cards . . . They should be applauded.

"From Hillsboro, Oregon, the Stevens family writes that they are fixing up their bikes to save energy as they do family errands. Bob Cantrell, a fourteen-year-old in Pasadena, California, gave up his stereo to save energy.

"Ten dollars' worth of seeds on a 25-by-30-foot plot will grow $290 worth of vegetables . . . there is still plenty of time to plant WIN gardens . . . We waste food, gasoline, paper, electricity, natural resources. As a matter of fact, we waste almost everything. One friend told me we could probably whip—just understand this—whip inflation with the contents of our trash cans. The first words I can remember in my dad's house were very simple but very direct: Clean up your plate before you get up from the table. And that is still pretty good advice.

"My twelfth and final point is an important one to every one of us: Guard your health. One of the worst wastes we have in America is days lost through sickness."

The President had been right about something in his address to Congress: the American people did want leadership. They expect the President to be their leader. They believe he is their leader. They listen to what he says—at least some of the people some of the time. Gerald Ford, who was used to not being listened to and clearly did not understand the power of his Presidential words, was not only telling the country to wear sweaters and turn down the heat, he was telling people to put off buying, not to use credit. He told them it would be a good idea to wait a while before "buying that new automobile." Well, a lot of people were doing what he told them. The country was in a recession already, which he denied every day, and it was getting worse, which he also denied. Factories and stores were reacting to sagging sales and Republican economic rhetoric by battening down their hatches— cutting back payrolls and inventories. Americans were losing their jobs, and Ford was talking about planting radishes in the back yard.*

It was not until after the 1974 congressional elections that the country heard for the first time from the White House that it was in a recession; until then Americans had only been hearing it from their bosses and their banks. Spokesman Ron Nessen, who was being asked every day whether the President agreed with economists who said a recession began some months ago, said on November 12: "New figures will probably indicate that we are moving into a recession . . . The President took this into account when he sent his economic message to Congress . . . the message is balanced between dealing with both problems, recession and inflation . . . There is some advance indication that industrial production apparently

---

* Ford's admonition not to use credit was not the only indication that he did not comprehend the power of his words as the President of the United States compared with the words of Congressman Ford. On October 9, at a press conference, he was asked for his reaction to Boston mayor Kevin White's request for U.S. marshals to help control demonstrations and violence that followed Federal court orders to bus black students into the white schools of South Boston. "The court decision in that case," he answered, "in my judgment, was not the best solution to quality education in Boston . . . I respectfully disagree with the judge's order." The President's words became a rallying cry for demonstrators, and the violence not only continued, but escalated.

163

has been slipping. There is evidence of unemployment continuing to increase."

Ignoring questions about whether it was a coincidence that the President waited until after the elections to discover the recession, Nessen said Ford still wanted to balance the 1976 budget, then added: "Almost every economist and other representative at the summit meetings indicated that large government spending was a main cause of inflation." For good measure, he added that a Harris poll indicated that 76 per cent of the American public believed "Federal spending is a major cause of inflation."

The public may have believed that—their President told it to them every day—but their President and his spokesman were distorting very recent history by mentioning economists, as most of them had said just the opposite. At the financial mini-summit, IBM vice-president David Grove had presented a computer study indicating that an immediate $10 billion cut in Federal spending would lower the rate of consumer price increases only 0.1 per cent by 1976, while causing unemployment to rise 0.5 per cent.

The new figures showed that unemployment was over 6 per cent and rising far faster than any economist, politician or labor leader had predicted, the Gross National Product was off 2.9 per cent for the year, and automobile sales were off a full 15 per cent. The President, however, seemed satisfied with his own tight-budget, surtax, WIN program. The next day, he and Mrs. Ford ceremoniously signed the WIN pledge, created by Benton & Bowles with the editing of the President himself: "I pledge to my fellow citizens that I will buy, when possible, only those products and services priced at or below present levels. I also promise to conserve energy and urge others to sign this pledge."

After signing, Ford joked that he should not even bother, pointing to his wife and saying: "She spends all the money." Then he sent letters to the nation's governors and mayors urging them to establish local WIN committees and begin signing up other inflation-fighters and energy-savers. More seriously, he added: "I see no justification for any major revisions [in this] finely tuned program."

New facts, for Ford, did not have the weight of old instincts and old Nixon advisers. Except for Hartmann's political input, Ford was dependent on the architects of Nixonomics for advice on whether or not their original advice was any good. Not surprisingly, OMB Director Roy Ash and the others advised him to stick it out and let the country take what they were sure would be a mild recession. The problem was that their thinking and Ford's rhetoric were almost certainly guaranteeing that the slump would continue to get worse.*

On November 6, Roy Ash, Nixon's old budget director and the former president of Litton Industries, began briefing the President on preparations for the Federal budget for fiscal 1976, the budget that would carry Ford almost through the end of Nixon's aborted term. Once again, it was a one-student seminar as Ash began: "Mr. President, I think you should steep yourself in some of the larger sorts of philosophical budget issues before you sit down and deal with specifics."

Ash then outlined his budget theories based on four premises. First, that Federal expenditures in terms of constant dollars or percentages of Gross National Product had not grown for the past six years—a fact at odds with Ford's usual "big spenders" campaign rhetoric. Second, the constant dollar cost of what he called "sovereign" functions of government—running agencies and national defense—was actually declining. Third, what he called "income redistribution" costs—

---

* Ford stuck stubbornly with "contained recession" policies until mid-January 1975, when unemployment had soared over 8 per cent and Bob Hartmann was warning him that American economics had become American politics and that his own hopes for election in 1976 depended on economic recovery in 1975. As late as December 11 he said, "If there are any among you who want me to take a 180-degree turn from inflation-fighting to recessionary pump-priming, they will be disappointed." Thirty days later, he turned, proposing massive income tax cuts to fight recession.

Social Security, Medicare, food stamps, revenue sharing—were increasing rapidly and absorbing "sovereign" savings. Fourth, the Federal government was at a crossroads because "sovereign" costs could no longer be cut to absorb mandated increases in Social Security and other "income redistribution."

The OMB director then concluded by stating that the President had three options in preparing the 1976 budget: (1) cut back legislatively mandated "income redistribution" program increases; (2) raise taxes; (3) increase the national debt with an unbalanced budget.

It was a simple, if debatable, analysis, and like many presented to Ford on different subjects, tended to lock his decision-making into options presented by Nixon's staff. Ford's political conditioning and the tenacious opportunism of the Nixon holdovers had an inevitable result—and that result was not a "Ford administration." Rather it was a Ford accommodation; as he had done in making his way in Congress, Ford accommodated himself to the situation as it was presented to him. The leader was being led by a group of men he had not selected and did not know particularly well—they just happened to be there when he arrived. Jerry Ford likes to "work with people," to get along with everyone, so . . .

"This has been very educational," the President said to Ash after the ninety-minute budget briefing. "I wish the country could hear this."

FOR the ordinary, hard-working middle-class American, travel is its own reward. It has all the appearances of work—even if you don't do anything but move purposefully. Moving, looking busy, satisfies the American work ethic, an eroding ethic in a society where more and more people seem unable to explain exactly what it is that they do to earn a living. I, for one, regularly meet apparently prosperous Americans who can't coherently answer the question, "What do you do?" Some of those I've met have impressive titles in the White House. One day we may be a nation of middlemen, community relations people and administrators, having completely outwitted Karl Marx who thought work had to be productive.

But who is to deny the genuine weariness and satisfaction of a man who began his labors at 7 A.M. in Los Angeles and ended with a couple of drinks with co-workers at midnight in Portland, Oregon? That was President Ford's busy day on November 1, 1974.

Travel is not only busyness, it's fun. Away from the office and the papers, the family—on the road, a man among men. Sinclair Lewis put George F. Babbitt on a train from Zenith to New York and saw it this way: "They were free, in a man's world, in the smoking compartment of the Pullman . . . The

167

small room, with its walls of ocher-colored steel, was filled mostly with the sort of men he classified as the Best Fellows You'll Ever Meet—Real Good Mixers."

Ford traveled 24,000 miles in his first hundred days as President, most of it campaigning for old Republican friends in the House. In many ways, his days in October and early November were not substantially different than they had been in earlier election years as House minority leader—except this time the accommodations were better, and people paid more attention.

The President, after all, is the symbol of our union and very real pride. It does not particularly matter symbolically who pops out of Air Force One, just as it does not matter who sits on the throne in Buckingham Palace at the moment. There is a difference, however. The Queen or King of England is only head of state. The President of the United States is head of state and head of government—it's a problem for Americans who love their country but not the government of the moment.

There is more than a bit of magic in their air whenever the President's plane approaches. There was on November 2, when a dot of black expanded into the silver jet in the perfect blue sky above the Continental Divide as the plane descended over the mountains, mesas and, finally, silhouetted horsemen, settling into the small airport outside Grand Junction, Colorado.

"There it is! There's Air Force One!" William Walter and David Hopkins, the Huntley-Brinkley of Grand Junction, told the listeners of KREX, The Voice of Intermountain West. "Here it comes, landing full flaps" . . . "It's touched down" . . . "It's only, maybe, I would guess 300 yards from us, Dave" . . . "It's turning toward us" . . . "They're rolling up two ramps, one to the front and one to the back. We're walking toward the plane. We're walking toward the plane now. Which ramp will the President use?" . . . "Probably the back, Bill" . . . "The President of the United States will be out any minute now . . ."

168

Unfortunately for KREX fans, the President was already out. He had come down the front ramp, as always, and Walter and Hopkins had just walked right by Gerald R. Ford.

It was something like the joke the President tried to tell two weeks earlier in Indianapolis. He began a speech there by saying that he was traveling around the country because his advisers said he needed more visibility. Then he was supposed to say he passed a lady in the hall who said, "You look familiar," and he helpfully answered, "Jerry Ford?" "No, but you're close," she replied.

Unhappily for Bob Orben, who wrote the joke, Ford fluffed it, telling the Indianapolis crowd that he answered, "I am Jerry Ford," and the lady in his version answered, "No, but you're closer."

Oh, well. Ford had entered the White House saying he would be too busy for political travel. The country, after all, was in a crisis. On August 14, Ford's sixth day as President, the Japanese government announced that he would visit their islands before the end of the year, and White House correspondents immediately asked whether the President would campaign at home. "The heavy schedule of speaking engagements that the Vice-President had laid on when he was Vice-President had to be stopped or aborted," said Jerry terHorst "The President feels that his most pressing problems are those that face him here in Washington, and I think his attitude at the present time is that the best politics of all is to be here attending to the affairs of the country, rather than traveling, making political speeches."

On August 30, terHorst announced that Ford planned "some political campaigning after Congress adjourns this year" and set the dates for four trips. Finally, there were twenty-three trips, sixteen of them before Congress adjourned.

This was my journal of the last campaign trips, covering 9,545 miles of the travels of the President of the United States from October 24 to November 2. It was, I suppose, not conventional journalism because journalism has limits. There is

no accepted technique that deals with what I saw happening.
Do you write:

Special to The New York Times

GRAND JUNCTION, Colorado, Nov. 2—President Ford had
nothing to say and said it badly today to a friendly and re-
spectful but slightly stunned crowd of 5,000.

Des Moines, Iowa, October 24

The basic Ford message is delivered from the steps of the
Iowa State House and at a Republican fund-raising lunch in
the Val Air Ballroom, across the street from the national headquarters of Roto-Rooter:

"I know there are some so-called experts who say the President ought to sit in the Oval Office and listen to bureaucrats
telling him what to do, yes or no, or sitting in the Oval Office
reading documents that are prepared by people in Washington.
I reject that advice. It is more important that I come to Des
Moines.

"Let me be quite categorical and explain as I see it why we
need tight-fisted members of the House and Senate to help us
in this battle against inflation.

"You might ask yourself, what can your vote accomplish?
The answer is very simple: It can send to the Congress men
and women who are not big spenders . . . I remind you a
government big enough to give us everything we want is a
government big enough to take from us everything we have."

The Ford rhetoric and faith in the American economic system seems unchanged from his congressional days—it is also
more than vaguely reminiscent of Herbert Hoover's—con-
firming for me, at least, that the economic summit meetings
were a charade for him, at least. Certainly the millions of
words he heard last month have not changed his mind about
anything. He still thinks the system will correct itself if left
alone.

On the flight to Des Moines, the President's press secre-

170

tary, Ron Nessen, tells reporters that Ford has no plans to visit Richard Nixon next week when he campaigns in California.

Chicago, Illinois, October 24

After being greeted by Mayor Richard Daley and Miss Teenage Chicago, Diane Weinbrenner, the President attends two Republican cocktail parties before sitting on the dais at the Illinois United Republican Fund dinner. He sits there an hour and thirteen minutes, smiling and applauding as a series of candidates predict that they are going to defeat the Democrats in Cook County.

Grand Rapids, Michigan, October 29

Breathes there a man with soul so dead who never to himself has said: Someday, I'm going to show them. Today, Gerald Ford returns to his home town for the first time as President of the United States.

The President's schedule, however, looks about the same as it has most days this month:

2:50 P.M. The President boards Army One and departs South Lawn enroute Andrews Air Force Base.

3:10 P.M. The President arrives Andrews Air Force Base, boards Air Force One and departs enroute Kent County Airport.

4:35 P.M. The President arrives Kent County Airport.

5:05 P.M. The President arrives Calder Plaza and proceeds to platform.

5:12 P.M. Welcoming remarks by Peter Secchia, master of ceremonies, and introduction of Mrs. Althea Bennett, who will present the President with a box of homemade cookies for Mrs. Ford.

171

5:25 P.M.	Presidential remarks.
5:45 P.M.	Presidential remarks conclude.
6:20 P.M.	The President arrives Hospitality Inn ballroom to attend informal GOP reception.
7:25 P.M.	The President is presented a Shrine fez by Irving and Shirley Talbert at Presidential Suite.
7:30 P.M.	The President meets with labor representatives at Presidential Suite.
7:45 P.M.	The President meets with Cliff Taylor and Bob Eastman, GOP Congressional District candidates.
8:27 P.M.	The President arrives Calvin College Fieldhouse.
8:55 P.M.	Presidential remarks.
9:15 P.M.	Presidential remarks conclude. (Note: The President accepts a wood carving of the Presidential seal by Ed Graverson and a painting by Paul Collins, local artists.)
9:35 P.M.	The President departs Calvin College via auto enroute Kent County Airport.
9:50 P.M.	At planeside, the President will be presented with a lifetime membership in the Fraternal Order of Police Lodge #97.
9:55 P.M.	The President boards Air Force One and departs Kent County Airport.
11:10 P.M.	The President arrives Andrews Air Force Base, boards Army One.
11:30 P.M.	The President arrives the South Lawn, the White House.

The homecoming seems surprisingly unemotional—or perhaps Ford and the people who knew him when are just stolid folk. It is a dreary, rainy night and the President says that "words are inadequate to express everything I feel deep down in my heart." Certainly his words are, and things aren't helped when he pledges "my heart, my soul, my conviction, my dedication" to the election of a congressional candidate named Paul Goebel, Jr., whom he later admits privately is something of a clod.

Lyman Parks, the mayor of Grand Rapids, opens the ceremonies by thanking Michigan Governor William Milliken for interrupting his busy schedule to come to town, but curiously, no speaker ever mention's Ford's schedule. The mayor presents the President with a replica of a table used by Lincoln, made by local furniture craftsmen, and only Ford realizes that the crowd of about 10,000 can't see the gift. He walks past several people on the platform to get to the table and hold it up for them. There are also a couple of dozen hostile signs in the Plaza, things like "But Jerry, You Endorsed Nixon, Too" and "Employees of Chrysler-Lyons-Trim Protest: Ford Said Don't Buy Cars."

The President's delivery is as flat and stumbling as usual, and the crowds give him far more applause before he speaks than after. At the Calvin College Republican rally, Christian High School cheerleaders are used to rehearse the crowd's cheering and applause for an hour before Ford arrives. The official White House transcript of his remarks is later edited to make a little more sense. The "as delivered" text, for instance, indicates the President said of World War II: "We got involved in a contest between freedom on the one hand and the effort on the part of some to subjugate people on the other." Actually he said, "We got involved in a contest between freedom on the one hand and liberty on the . . . and . . . and . . . and . . . the effort to . . . to the effort on the part of some to subjugate people on the other."

Back at Kent County Airport, however, there are several hundred people waiting to see the President in a downpour. With Secret Service agents scrambling to hold an umbrella over him, Ford sloshes through mud and small rain lakes to shake hands for twenty minutes, saying, "Hi . . . Hi . . . Good to see you . . . Thank you . . . Thank you." On the

173

plane back to Washington, Nessen says Ford has learned that Nixon is in critical condition in Long Beach but the new President has no plans to visit his predecessor in California.

Sioux City, Iowa, October 31

On the flight from Washington to Sioux City, Nessen says the President has no plans to visit Nixon tomorrow in California. The press secretary also emphasizes that there has been no change in United States policy toward Palestinian refugees, even though the President, at a news conference the day before, had seemed to back off the U.S. position that all negotiations on Israeli-occupied territories on the west bank of the Jordan River must include only Israel and Jordan, by saying: "We, of course, feel there must be a movement toward settlement between Israel and Egypt on the one hand, between Israel and Jordan or the PLO on the other."

Whatever the President meant by that—he seemed to be equating the legitimacy of Jordan and the Palestine Liberation Organization—the White House press corps doesn't take the thing particularly seriously. The unstated assumption is that Henry Kissinger handles American foreign policy. One senior correspondent says: "What the hell, it was just Jerry talking about things he doesn't understand."

On the ground in Sioux City, Don Stone, the public relations director of the Northwestern State Bank, is rehearsing crowd cheers: "Now when I say, 'Ladies and gentlemen, the President of the United States,' I want you to . . ."

Ford tells the crowd not to pay any attention to a Des Moines headline that says "Ford Has No Farm Plan." He says he does have a plan and begins to list a series of existing laws and agreements "I will strictly enforce."

Los Angeles, California, October 31

At 7:16 P.M. Nessen announces that the President has just telephoned Mrs. Richard Nixon in Long Beach and said: "I don't want to push, but would it help if I came down there?"

Mrs. Nixon replied: "I cannot think of anything that would do him more good." Nessen says Ford is checking to see if his schedule allowed him time. In fact, there has always been a suspiciously blank spot on the schedule for the morning of November 1.

After meetings with Governor Ronald Reagan and a couple of cocktail parties, the President goes to a $250- and $500-a-plate Republican dinner at the Century Plaza Hotel. It's a rather classy affair, and as I walk into the hotel, a man in a Cadillac asks, "Do you park the cars around here?"

The President sits on the dais for an hour and thirty-eight minutes listening to a succession of local Republicans, Bob Hope and the music of Manny Harmon, who says Ford asked him to play the songs from *Oklahoma*.

Hope is very funny, perhaps closer to the truth than he knows: "The President and Kissinger are both early risers. Whoever gets to the airport first gets the plane." On Ford's plane, the press is convinced that Ford is traveling to avoid the Oval Office, just as a businessman travels to avoid his "In" basket or a reporter to avoid his editors. There is no way Ford can do any thinking about the economy, energy or anything else on this schedule, unless Bob Hope and Manny Harmon are up there talking to him about the balance of payments deficit.

Nessen, who is being battered with questions about who's running the country, says, "Look, he enjoys this. He's having a good time." Ford himself adds that he enjoys the food at political dinners. He certainly seems to. He is one of the very few people in the room actually eating it. Everyone else eats before or after—one theory being that the chicken and roast beef at political dinners are Army surplus.

Los Angeles, California, November 1

At 8:15 A.M., Nessen announces that Ford will leave at 9:35 to visit Nixon. The press is a little testy about the Nixon game, and the following questioning ensues:

175

Q. Ron, did the possibility of a visit to the former President first arise last night when the President called Mrs. Nixon?

A. That is correct.

Q. Why were the Secret Service over there the day before that checking it out?

A. Bob, I am told that was the Secret Service detail assigned to the former President, and they were simply making preparations for his stay in the hospital.

Q. Ron, was there some reason, then, that a hole was left in the President's schedule this morning?

A. So he could catch up on his sleep due to the time change, Russ.

"Did you have a good night?" Ford asks Nixon at Long Beach Memorial Hospital. Nixon replies, "None of the nights are too good." In talking about the hospital visit, Ford always refers to Nixon as "the President."

Fresno, California, November 1

There are worse public speakers than Gerald Ford. Representative Robert Mathias is one. It's shattering for everyone who remembers Bob Mathias of Tulare, California, winning the decathalon in the 1948 London Olympics, but Congressman Mathias is reading slowly when he says: "I'm proud to be your representative. Frankly, I'm anxious to get back to work . . . Please get out and vote."

Ford follows that with an inadvertent double entendre: "This big valley . . . to serve its people in Congress it produces big men, mentally and otherwise in Bob Mathias."

The President is having even more trouble than usual with the language. He says judgment as "judge-e-ment," almost with an Italian accent; athlete becomes "ath-e-lete, with the same accent; séance becomes "see-ance," and the capital of California is someplace called "Sacer-emento."

"This guy's going to Vladivostok?" says George Murphy of the San Francisco *Chronicle*.

176

The President's staff is furious when Air Force One lands in Portland—Ford has been used by someone named Diarmuid O'Scannlain.

O'Scannlain is the Republican candidate for Congress in Oregon's First District, and he appeared in Fresno to hitch a ride north on Air Force One. He wanted to talk to Ford and did for a couple of minutes; then he ran back to the press section of Air Force One and said he had just told the President of the United States that he was wrong to pardon Nixon and wrong to propose a 5 per cent income tax surcharge. "Son of a bitch" is the nicest thing anyone official had to say about O'Scannlain.

On the flight, Ford also looks over a cable from Kissinger outlining the secretary of State's speech next week to the World Food Conference in Rome. The President does not review all Kissinger speeches, Nessen says, but he does see "major" ones, and the press secretary says the incident is proof that the President is the President no matter where he travels.

After the usual round of Republican receptions, Ford heads for the annual auction of the Oregon Museum of Science and Industry, a black-tie fund-raising affair in the Portland Coliseum. Boats and even airplanes are being auctioned off to a handsome, champagne-drinking crowd that seems pretty recession-proof. The President is there twenty-five minutes. He autographs two footballs that bring $2,700 each, and two pairs of his cufflinks go for $11,000 to a lumber dealer and $10,000 to a food distributor.

It is a high good time. Ford is bouncing around like a kid, and when the bidding on the first football reaches $500, he grabs the microphone and says: "Double it, and I'll center it to you." Which is exactly what the center of the 1934 Michigan team does—after moving around when he suddenly realizes three dozen camera lenses are focused on what his quarterback used to see. When the cufflink bidding starts

177

going crazy, Ron Nessen exclaims: "Jesus, I have a desk drawer filled with Presidential Seal Cufflinks." Finally, an auto parts dealer pays $1,100 for the chair Ford had sat on for a moment.

A happy and loose President gets looser next door where the National Basketball Association's Portland Trailblazers are playing. He roars with laughter when Bill Walton, the Portland center, returns to the bench after blowing a shot and growls in the general direction of the President three feet away: "Fuck!"

Salt Lake City, Utah, November 2

Radio and television are waiting, of course, when Ford arrives at Salt Lake City International Airport at 10:35 A.M. Howard Cook of KSXH radio sees it this way:

"The President of the United States is not just President Ford, a Republican. He is an institution. He is the most powerful man in the world. You say: what about the Russians? They have the same power we have, but there it takes more than one man to pull the trigger. Here we're set up so that one man can do the job. He would never dream of doing it, of course, but it's within his power."

The man with the power is introduced to 8,000 people at the University of Utah by Jake Garn, the mayor of Salt Lake City and Republican candidate for the U.S. Senate, who tells a charming and revealing story of a meeting between fourteen mayors and Ford just five days after he succeeded Nixon:

"We were just standing around talking and somehow the President slipped into the room and came up behind me and said, 'Hi, Jake, how are things in Salt Lake City?' When the meeting was over, someone asked, 'Is there anything we can do for you, Mr. President?' He said: 'Go home and pray for me. This is a very big job.'"

Ford's speech is the usual, with one exception—he's heckled hard by a dozen young men behind a sign that says: "We were

178

good enough to fight in your war—what about G.I. Education benefits?" There have been Vietnam veterans at every stop with the same demands for an expanded G.I. Bill for their war. After the speech, Nessen goes into the crowd to bring three of the vets behind the stage to meet the President. There isn't exactly a meeting of the minds, but at least it's a meeting, and Ford hears from somebody who isn't a Republican congressman or captain of industry.

"I'm not in a position to say yes or no until it gets down to the White House," the President says.

"Don't you have a stand on it?" one of the vets says.

"Wait a minute," Ford says, "Some of us served four years. The entitlement in World War II and Korea, which you want equality with, gives you nine more months than the sixteen million who served in the other drafts."

"There's a very good reason for it . . ."

"Now, now, wait just a minute," Ford interrupts. "And, in addition, there's a loan program that has to be analyzed. Now the student loan program we've had under NDEA has had a very bad repayment record."

"That's your era," the veteran says. "Those are your people that are not paying it back. That's not us."

"Well, I'm going to take a look at it," Ford says, "and we'll do the best. Thank you. Nice to see you." He does not tell the young man he has already approved an action memo recommending administration opposition to the veterans' benefits.

Grand Junction, Colorado, November 2

Diane Poster, a pretty twenty-year-old blonde, is the Mesa College Homecoming Queen, and the President is there to crown her before 5,000 people and twenty high school bands on the Lincoln Park Baseball Field. "A college homecoming is a happy time," he says, "and I wish Meesa College . . ."

The crowd lets out an embarrassed little gasp at the mispronunciation, but Ford recovers quickly "Messa College."

179

"Oh! Mesa?" the President says. "Well, we have some community names out in Michigan all of you could not pronounce either. I love you anyhow." He gets a laugh by pretending to write down Miss Poster's phone number.

As far as I know there is not a reporter on the trip that does not personally like Ford. But it has not been an inspiring month and the talk is getting brutal. A first-timer on the Ford trail asks an important White House correspondent, "Hey, Nixon was 'Searchlight,' what's Ford's Secret Service code name?"

"Dummy!" says the senior man.

His fellow travelers are routinely calling the President "Bozo" or "Bozo the Clown." On the flight from Grand Junction, a well-known political reporter almost shouts to his companions: "I can't believe this. There is no way I can get what's going on into the paper. He's Lennie. I'm telling you he's Lennie in *Of Mice and Men*. I can just hear him at the hospital with Nixon, 'Tell me again about the rabbits, Dick.'"

Driving into Grand Junction, we see two little girls in pigtails standing on a little rise with a pony. Between them, they hold a long, hand-painted sign that says "Pardon. Bah!"

It's time for farm talk, and as he often does in steer country, he begins by talking about cows: "I suspect there are some dairy farmers in this group. How many are here?"

One guy yells out.

Then the President starts talking about the unfairness of American farmers having to compete with foreign farmers who are subsidized by their governments:

"You know we, as Americans, like competition," he says. "I don't mind a German or a Dutchman or a Frenchman competing with me on an equal basis, but I will be doggoned if I want the government to subsidize the product he is trying to sell to the American people. We will challenge him on the open fields, head to head, and we will do all right."

To a city boy, the message finally got through: No country but the United States has the right to subsidize farmers or limit imports.

180

He closes with a civics lesson that has overtones that are almost Freudian: "You know we have three great branches of this government of ours . . . We have a strong President, supposedly in the White House. We have a strong Congress, supposedly in the legislative branch. We have a strong Supreme Court, supposedly heading the judiciary system."

Wichita, Kansas, November 2

While the President visits two Republican receptions and a Shriners meeting, David Owen, the lieutenant governor of Kansas, entertains 4,000 more waiting Republicans at the Century II Convention Center. "They tell me I have to fill a few more minutes before the President arrives. Well, I hate to tell Polack jokes, but these are Polack stories . . ."

Senator Robert Dole introduces the President, pointing out that "the last three Presidents have been destroyed—Kennedy, Johnson and Nixon—granted the last two may have contributed to that to some degree."

This one, Gerald Ford, spoke for twenty-eight minutes. When the transcript of his remarks was prepared, I said to someone on the White House staff: "You know the whole first page doesn't really make any sense."

"Wait till you see the second page," he answered.

On the flight from Wichita back to Washington, exhausted reporters look over the schedule for the President's next campaign. On November 17, he will take the road show to Japan, Korea and Russia. "Wait till the Russians get a load of this," someone says. "When they thought Kennedy was a clown in Vienna, they put missiles in Cuba. This time it might be Long Island."

Air Force One lands at Andrews Air Force Base early on Sunday, November 3, and the President of the United States is back at the White House at 1:15 A.M.

The press plane touched down at Andrews about an hour later. The tribal ceremonies over for a while, thirty tired reporters headed for home, hearth and woman. Like a lot of young newspapermen, I was once told by a city editor that the lead of a story is what you tell your wife when she asks you what went on that day. I am willing to bet that on that particular late night what reporters were telling their wives was a hell of a lot different from the stories they were writing that began, "President Ford today said . . ."

What did I say at home? "The President of the United States is a very ordinary man. Just another pol." Then I added that our last President was a recluse and this one can't stand being alone.

ON ELECTION NIGHT, November 5, the President joined Bob Hartmann, Don Rumsfeld, Roy Ash and a few other White House regulars in the Roosevelt Room to watch returns come in on three color televisions. "Is there anything from the Fifth?" Ford asked when he arrived at ten o'clock. Someone said that Paul Goebel, Jr., the Republican candidate for the old Ford seat in Grand Rapids, was running behind Democrat Richard vander Veen.

"That's okay. I think we can still win it," Ford said, explaining voting patterns in the district and saying that the Democratic vote usually comes in early. But in Grand Rapids and almost everywhere else, the Democratic vote just kept coming in—vander Veen won with 55 per cent of the total. The Democrats won 299 of the 435 seats in the House of Representatives, and there was not a single winner among the House candidates Ford had campaigned for. In the new Senate the Democrats would have sixty-one seats; five of the men Ford appeared for won.*

* The President later eased the pain for many of his defeated friends, appointing Republican ex-senators and ex-congressmen as ambassadors, assistant secretaries, deputy administrators, commissioners, consultants and other patronage positions that make electoral politics less risky than it looks.

183

The official White House statement on the results emphasized that the election could not be interpreted as a referendum on the Ford administration because most of the Republicans Ford campaigned for really never had a chance. It would have been impolite to point out that if that was true, the President had been deliberately wasting his own time or kidding himself and the country for the past month.

Unofficially and ironically, there was something like a sense of relief around the White House that the thing was over. One Ford man said confidentially that the election actually helped Ford because the results had finally evicted the political ghost of Richard Nixon. "From now on," he said, "it's a Ford administration." The same man, however, had said the same thing after the Nixon pardon, and after Alexander Haig left, and after Ford presented his economic program to Congress—and he and others said it again after Ford presented a completely different economic package to a new Congress in January. It was, in the words of his own men repeated in newspapers and on television, as if Gerald Ford were a fairy-tale hero who had become a prince overnight—or was about to become one.

Ten days later, as Ford approached his hundredth day in office and the traditional time for evaluating the performance of a new administration, the White House released its official version of what Gerald Ford had accomplished as President of the United States. "On Saturday, November 16, President Ford will mark his first hundred days in office," the three-page statement began. "From the outset, President Ford set a tone of stability and continuity in foreign policy, openness and candor in domestic affairs, cooperation and reasonableness in his dealings with Congress."

"A hallmark of the Ford administration in all fields," it said at the closing, "has been the openness and candor President Ford committed his administration to from the beginning."

In between, these were the listed achievements: personally presided over an "unprecedented" Economic Summit; pro-

184

posed an "action" program to attack spiraling prices and other economic weaknesses; ordered a price-fixing investigation in the food industry; appealed to citizens to voluntarily cut back fuel consumption; "dispatched Secretary of State Kissinger on a number of overseas missions"; met with more than sixty ambassadors, five "major" labor leaders and representatives of national women's organizations, the National Governors Conference, National Association of County Officials, U.S. Conference of Mayors, civil rights groups and the Congressional Black Caucus, National Association of Manufacturers, and the U.S. Chamber of Commerce; worked with Congress "in a spirit of conciliation and compromise" and signed legislation passed by Congress concerning education, housing, pension reform, campaign reform and energy problem-solving; persuaded General Motors to reduce car prices $54; limited White House access to income tax returns; ordered conditional Vietnam amnesty; helped shape a $12 billion mass transit bill; "moved to cut" the 1975 budget by $5 billion, and aimed for a balanced 1976 budget.

There was something a bit sad about the document. It was supposed to have the feel of history, but it was inadequate even as public relations. It is hard to imagine any other President of the United States listing a meeting with representatives of the National Association of County Officials as an "accomplishment."

The first hundred days of a President's administration have had a symbolic, almost mystical, importance in the United States since Franklin D. Roosevelt's New Deal was launched in one hundred productive days in 1933. "We became again an organized nation," wrote Walter Lippmann at the time, "confident of our own power to provide for our own security and to control our own destiny."

Like Roosevelt, Ford came to power at a confusing and dangerous time when Americans were no longer confident about controlling their own destiny. The brutality, the stupidity and the dishonesty of Vietnam, the shocks of Watergate, and the profoundly disturbing realization that their great country did not have endless resources and potential had done something to what used to be called the American spirit—the boundless optimism about the future and progress, and unlimited, almost irrational faith in national self bred into most Americans. The times again cried for leadership, not so much to restore the optimism and faith, which were always tinged with unreality, but to offer a credible vision of a more realistic national future and the means and will to realize a destiny less than manifest.

But all that these times could produce was a Jerry Ford, and he was a fair end product of the American political system. He had been nurtured, conditioned and honored by that system. He succeeded within it by finding and being the least objectionable alternative. Ford and others not very different from him have succeeded in the American political system on an inoffensive track that almost guarantees failure if they reach their original goals, positions of leadership. The conditioning becomes the condition: leaders who cannot lead.

The most extraordinary thing about Ford's ascension to the Vice-Presidency and then the Presidency was the lack of questioning from his peers about his abilities and capabilities. Except for a handful of liberals who disagreed with Ford's ideology, not with his qualities, the political leaders of the nation, Republican and Democrat, rose to publicly second the nomination of the man from Grand Rapids. I remember only one politician, Representative Michael Harrington of Massachusetts, rising to question Ford's fitness for the highest national office, and he was greeted with the enthusiasm usually reserved for drunks in church when he said: "After all, we are undertaking a rather historic mission. For the first time, the Congress of the United States will be substituting its judgment for the judgment of the people in the selection of a man who may soon assume the Presidency. . . . I share the widely held perception that Jerry Ford is an honest and decent man . . . But honesty and decency are not enough. We also

186

must look for proven qualities of leadership and an ability to serve as a focal point around which a country, a troubled country as I view it, can rally."

Harrington was scorned by his fellows because on congressional terms—and the Congress has produced five of the last six Presidents—Jerry Ford had demonstrated leadership, he had succeeded in winning a position of congressional leadership. Ford himself could see no difference between a leadership position and leadership. After being in the Oval Office for five months, he found few differences between congressional leadership and national leadership.

"The experience, the training I had in the Congress has been invaluable," Ford told the Washington *Post* in a long interview at the beginning of 1975. "We have been going through the same process in the development of a plan for our energy program, or the economy program, the same way you almost do it in Congress. You listen to Bill Simon, to Arthur Burns, to Alan Greenspan. They have ideas, and you sort of—well, you have to make a judgment—you mesh here or you modify there. The only difference is, when you're in this office, among people on your staff or in your administration, if you make the decision it's supposed to stick. In the Congress, you don't have quite that authority. But the process isn't too much different.

"The experiences, again, I had in Congress I think were helpful in giving me the way of working with people in the executive branch, the same as you have to work with people in the legislative branch."

"Working with people," however, is not leadership. Taking them or making them go someplace is. Harry Truman, whose bust was in the office where Ford was speaking, had said: "You know what makes leadership? It is the ability to get men to do what they don't want to do and like it." And you can't do that without sometimes telling people what they don't want to hear.

Gerald Ford, conditioned not to offend, did not know how

to inspire, persuade or force people to go anyplace. He did not have the skills and when he tried to imitate them, as he did in pushing the WIN program, all he could offer was a parody of leadership. More than that, Ford did not know the someplace he wanted to take or make the American people go, because he did not know where they had been in the last few years. Ford had substantial gaps in his knowledge of issues like the economy and energy, but the more tragic gaps and the ones that had graver implications were in understanding —he did not understand Vietnam and Watergate.

Ford happened to be the President when the government of South Vietnam fell to Communist forces in the spring of 1975, after a fifteen-year American investment of 55,000 lives and $150 billion. His reaction—under the almost manic prodding of Kissinger who had negotiated "peace with honor" in Vietnam—as the Communists drove toward Saigon was to ask Congress to appropriate another $1 billion in aid even as the South Vietnamese army was abandoning billions of dollars worth of American arms in panicked retreat.

His words as the South Vietnamese government fell, often spoken as he came off golf courses during a Palm Springs vacation, were as totally divorced from the reality of America as that rich oasis is from the desert around it.* Most of the Americans he was speaking to were fed up, disgusted; polls indicated that as many as 80 per cent of voting Americans were against any kind of new aid to Southeast Asia, and those feelings went years-deep. The American people had learned a lot from Vietnam, learned the hard way that as powerful as the United States was, it could not necessarily impose its will at will—and learned that their government had lied and lied to them again those fifteen years.

"What kind of people are we?" asked Kissinger and Ford, trying to focus the issue of last-minute aid to South Vietnam as

* The Fords, incidentally, did not go back to Sunnylands and the bossy servants of Walter Annenberg. They paid $100-a-day rent, their own money, to use another friend's $350,000 home.

a test of American will and commitment to allies, even allies who seemed unwilling to fight for themselves. Well, we are not fools all of the time, and if our will was broken it was not by Asian guerrillas but by the deception of our own leadership, by the years of lying by Presidents Kennedy, Johnson and Nixon, Secretaries of State Dean Rusk and Kissinger, and Secretaries of Defense Robert McNamara and Melvin Laird. And by House Minority Leader Gerald Ford, who said there was no lying when he knew of secret American bombing of Cambodia.

But Ford seemed to have learned nothing from Vietnam. His rhetoric and thought were at least a decade out of date. In 1966, Americans might have believed the South Vietnamese were "fighting for their freedom," but when the President was using that same phrase in April 1976, Americans could see South Vietnamese soldiers on television every night and they were were not fighting, they were running and knocking down women and children to climb aboard rescue ships and helicopters. And Americans on the rescue vehicles were doing the same thing, kicking away helpless hands. What kind of people were we, indeed—and what kind of leadership had maneuvered us into corners where we struck like rats!

But people, at least the people I saw in April 1975, did not seem particularly angry with President Ford. It was worse than that, far worse: they were laughing at the President of the United States. That nice man who moved into the White House when they threw out Nixon, he wanted more aid for Vietnam, he couldn't be serious!

Whether or not Minority Leader Ford knew more about Watergate and the dark nature of the Nixon White House than he has ever admitted—he did, after all, meet with President Nixon at least once a week and more regularly with other Watergate principals—it is clear that he never comprehended the nature of the scandal or its effect on the American psyche. Certainly Ford did not understand Nixon's "true crime," as

189

defined by Theodore White, the crime of destroying "the myth that binds America together . . . that somewhere in American life there is at least one man who stands for law, the President." I prefer the word "faith" to "myth," but that is beside the point, which is that because Ford could not understand the crime, he was incapable of doing what he wanted to do—restore the faith of Americans in their President and in themselves.

If Ford had understood, he would have realized that to "close the book on Watergate," as he said he wanted to do with the Nixon pardon, he had to demand, at the very least, a statement of guilt and contrition from the former President. Instead, the new President asked for nothing and Nixon volunteered a vague statement about anguish over "my mistakes." Nixon did not make mistakes; he was a criminal who subverted the Constitution of the United States, our supreme article of faith and law.

Ford's decision not to clean out the Nixon White House was not only foolish for his own purposes, it was an insult to the nation. And a lot of the "cleaning" that was announced was merely cosmetic—H. R. Haldeman's most trusted assistant, Lawrence Higby, one of the very few people aware of the installation of the Oval Office taping system, for instance, was hidden away as a $38,000-a-year "consultant" to the Office of Management and Budget. Did Ford really believe, as he said he did, that the issue was kindness and consideration toward employees, that he should not throw out men who may have had nothing to do with Watergate?

If he was sensitive to the feelings of each Nixon man, Ford's insensitivity to the nation and the truth of Watergate was revealed in the letters he wrote acknowledging the resignations of Richard Nixon's two principal speech writers, Raymond Price and Patrick Buchanan.

To Price, he wrote on November 15: "History will one day record the important achievements of these past years." The implication of the letter, of course, was that contemporary judgments of the Nixon years were wrong. We shall see, Mr. President.

To Buchanan, whom he was willing to make an ambassador until he realized confirmation was impossible, he wrote: "I want to thank you for your great dedication to the nation . . . Throughout the Nixon administration you were among President Nixon's most effective, articulate and courageous advisers." I would not argue Pat Buchanan's dedication to his country, but among the advice he offered Nixon was the strong suggestion he destroy the Watergate tapes before they could be used by investigating committees or the Justice Department. On a personal level, the President was thanking the man who had ten months earlier written the Atlantic City speech in which Vice-President Ford said talk of impeaching Nixon was "a massive propaganda campaign" to allow organized labor to "dominate the nation." No hard feelings, Pat —that's why people think Jerry Ford is such a nice guy.*

The last official act of Ford's hundred days, in fact, was a letter, actually an exchange of letters, with Peter Flanigan, Nixon's Mr. Fixit, who asked that his name be withdrawn as the nominee as ambassador to Spain because of "the current political climate." Ford answered the letter on November 16, expressing his deepest regret and the opinion that "you have served your country with the greatest distinction."

At 9:30 on the morning of his 101st day as President of the United States, Gerald Ford left on an eight-day tour of summit meetings in Japan, Korea and the Soviet Union. Before going, he read the Washington *Post* and saw a cartoon reprinted from the Dayton *Daily News*. The drawings, by Mike Peters, show a husband and wife drinking coffee with their faces hidden by their morning papers.

* Ford's press secretary, Ron Nessen, resisted the impulse to be a nice guy about Father John McLaughlin, the Nixon speech writer who intended to become a White House fixture. On October 2, Nessen called McLaughlin in and told him he was fired. When Nessen announced at a briefing that McLaughlin would be leaving on October 15, a reporter yelled out, "What year?"

"That does it," the husband says. "Look at this month's cost of living increase . . . Somebody better tell the President to get off his duff and start giving us some answers."

"You're the President, dear," says his wife.

"Oh yeah, right, right . . ."

6

The Politician as Usual

Politicians don't mean badly; most of the time they don't mean anything.

Walter Lippmann

MR. PRESIDENT," Ford was asked after his first hundred days were over, "the polls show that while you yourself remain personally popular, the American people would like to see a greater sense of urgency in meeting the energy problems and in meeting the economic problems in this country . . . How do you respond?"

"How much more can a President do than to recommend legislation," Ford told the editors of *Newsweek,* "have his people do their very best to talk to committee members, to chairmen, to the leadership? . . . I do not think you are going to get a breakthrough in legislation in the field of energy until you get a brownout or a blackout. I think it is just that pragmatic. You won't get deregulation of natural gas until the cutbacks in natural gas in Washington and in New York and New England start to hurt people or hurt jobs. That is a bad commentary on our system, perhaps, but that is the way we act, right or wrong."

What's a President to do? Perhaps the bad and sad commentary is that we tolerate a system that produces leaders who act that way, right or wrong. And that is the system American leaders want and have helped create—a safe circle of honored and titled men and women pointing their fingers.

197

It's Congress's responsibility. No, it's the President's responsibility. It's the press. It's the bureaucrats. It's the people, they won't care until there's a blackout. Or, it's nobody's fault—things have just gotten too big, too complicated.

On energy, Ford first pointed at the public with the WIN program—volunteerism. That collapsed, partly because the leaders of the country had made no real attempt to educate their people about the dimensions and implications of the energy dilemma—hardly surprising, since *the* national leader, President Ford, was essentially ignorant of the scope and danger of what he was talking about when he threw around the phrase "energy crisis."

Then, after briefings during a ten-day end-of-the-year skiing vacation, Ford did announce an energy program of sorts on January 13, 1975. The President imposed a one-dollar-a-barrel import fee on foreign oil coming into the United States and said he would continue to raise the fee until Congress came up with comprehensive energy legislation. It's your responsibility now!

Congress, predictably, came up with nothing for months and months except attacks on Ford for accomplishing nothing but raising consumer prices of fuel and heating oil. But Ford had accomplished something: he was winning the battle of the blame. Politically, the President was ahead—his popularity began to climb in national opinion polls—even though nothing substantial had happened.

It was a classic game, but a bit dangerous. Spreading blame, like throwing mud, can get both sides dirty—the stuff splatters. Blameless politics would be the best of all possible games for professionals. And theories of blameless politics did come out of the Vietnam war—power without responsibility, irresponsibility without accountability. Apologists for five presidents and ten Congresses began writing and saying that the war was not a product of leadership but of bureaucracy, faceless generals and planners hidden somewhere across the Potomac River in the Pentagon. Then Richard Goodwin, a resident intellectual and speech writer for Presidents Kennedy and Johnson, refined those arguments into a Tolstoyan analysis. If Vietnam is a disaster, he wrote, "there will be no act of madness, no single villain on whom to discharge guilt; just the flow of history."

Goodwin, a liberal Democrat, and Ford, a conservative Republican, might disagree on many things, but they found common ground in that defense of American leadership. The President, after a quick and clumsy attempt to blame Democrats in Congress for the disintegration of the South Vietnamese government, asserted that no blame should be assessed, that nothing could gained by pondering the lessons of Vietnam: "The war is over. The lessons of the past have been learned." He took the same line on Watergate: "The book is closed . . . We must look ahead."

Ford, in fact, had always displayed a certain fondness for a political world without specific villains. His criticisms were always creatively vague, inoffensive. He questioned South Vietnamese decision-making in the final days of the war while praising the maker of those decisions, President Thieu. He criticized the Committee to Re-elect the President for Watergate while absolving President Nixon and CREEP officials. He attacked "Congress" and "Democrats" while praising Speaker Carl Albert and Senate Majority Leader Mike Mansfield. And always he blamed "big spenders," "the bureaucracy" or just "people" or "the system, right or wrong."

That is the practiced rhetoric of the least objectionable alternative. It's habit-forming. When talking about his football experience a few years ago, Ford said centers in his single-wing playing days had more to do than their counterparts in modern T-formation football. "The center was not just the guy who stuck the ball in the quarterback's hands," he said. *"I don't mean to be critical,* but I think that is why you see so many bad passes from center on punts and field goals nowadays."

By early 1975, it was obvious to Ford's men in the White

House that their boss was looking too much like what he was, good old Jerry, the man without enemies. Meetings began to plot strategy to make Ford look like a leader in fact as well as title. One internal memo on the President's election prospects in 1976 focused almost entirely on the use of the first-person singular, urging the President to say "I," "me" and "my" and to stop referring to advisers, particularly Secretary of State Henry Kissinger—"You have to establish forcefully that *you* are the President!" One result was that when a United States air-sea armada recaptured an American merchant ship, the *Mayagüez,* after it had been seized off the coast of Southeast Asia by Cambodian patrol boats, Ford's first words in announcing the successful operation on national television were: "At *my* direction . . ."

The White House's make-Ford-a-leader committees, headed informally by chief-of-staff Donald Rumsfeld, came to two conclusions: Kissinger had to be downgraded, and there had to be a Presidential confrontation with Congress, the one institution guaranteed to make practically anyone look forceful. (The anti-Kissinger strategy also had an attractive fringe benefit for Rumsfeld—Rummy wanted the secretary of State's job.)

Like many of the many little plots inside the Ford White House, the *putsch* against Kissinger originated and operated at a level below the President. Ford himself was unable or unwilling to stop it; and some of his best friends thought it was inability, a basic inability to handle personal confrontation. "What does being a nice guy mean?" said one of the President's friends. "It means that you don't make other people uncomfortable. Maybe that you can't bear to make other people uncomfortable. Jerry just can't seem to bring himself to call in Rumsfeld or Hartmann and say, 'Look, I know what you're doing and I want it stopped!' "

This time it was Rumsfeld who was methodically gathering the kind of control that H. R. Haldeman and Alexander Haig had before him. Rummy was the prince behind what

200

John Osborne of *The New Republic* described as "the claque of White House assistants who continue to use every available occasion to further the notion that the President is deliberately downgrading Henry Kissinger and anyone else who may compete with Mr. Ford for media credit in foreign polity matters."

The "high White House source" stories about the President's reduced reliance on Kissinger or displeasure with the secretary echoed Hartmann's leak campaign against Haig six months earlier. That tried and true technique of image-depletion provided some interesting insights into American press, President and polity—the press was being used, again; there was implied disdain for Ford's ability to act on his own without the manipulation of his staff, and there was the demonstration of how often image was reality in Washington, where stories do not have to be true as long as they are published. Politicians like to denounce "Madison Avenue techniques," perhaps because they know Pennsylvania Avenue techniques can be more clever by half.

Congress, of course, is a big, slow-moving target—a Zeppelin in a sky of darts—easy for a reporter, easier for a President. Pettiness. pomposity and hypocrisy drift through the halls of Capitol Hill, and if decency and eloquence occasionally rise from the fog, as they did finally during the Nixon impeachment debates in the House, self-interest is the glue that binds Congress together. Less than a year after Nixon was pilloried for claiming "executive privilege" to cover his wrongdoing, the Senate quietly voted to refuse to release any financial records to the state of Florida for possible use in the bribery prosecution of former Senator Edward Gurney. Release, said the leaders of both parties, would "jeopardize the whole system of senatorial disclosure."

But even with Congress as the opposition, President Ford had not filled out the leader-of-men image his staff was pumping up. He had less success leading Congress than any new President in recent history. After taking over from Nixon, Ford won 58 per cent of the 122 congressional votes on which there was a clear White House position in the 93rd Congress. That record compared badly with the 80 to 90 per cent win records scored by Presidents Eisenhower, Kennedy, Johnson and Nixon in their first congressional confrontations—it was even worse than the 60 per cent scored by Nixon on 136 votes during the traumatic last eight months of his Presidency.*

Ford made a final pitch for "a new partnership" in his State of the Union address to the 94th Congress, saying, "Some people question their government's ability to make hard decisions and stick with them . . . They expect Washington politics as usual."

"Some people" were not surprised. The new partnership quickly deteriorated into the old blame-throwing—Washington's indelicate description of the status quo is "the usual pissing match"—with the Democratic Congress forcing the Republican President to sign, reluctantly, tax-rebate and economic-recovery legislation that would lead to an $80 billion deficit in the 1975–76 Federal budget, and Ford putting the divided Democrats on the defensive when they had trouble putting together a comprehensive energy policy.

Government in the middle of 1975 was a stalemate and politics were the usual. But that was not necessarily bad for Gerald Ford. He was the only President we had, traveling royally around the world, press and television at his heels (actually fifty yards behind his heels most of the time) send-

* Elected Presidents and elevated Vice-Presidents, like Johnson, have traditionally been very successful in their first "honeymoon" dealings with the legislative branch. According to *Congressional Quarterly* tabulations, the win records of previous Presidents, "if the President or his aides made a specific indication of his wishes before the vote was taken," were Eisenhower, with a Democratic Congress—88 per cent; Kennedy—82 per cent; Johnson, taking over in the middle of the 88th Congress—87 per cent; Nixon, with a Democratic Congress in 1969—80 per cent. During Ford's first five months in office, Republicans voted with him only 51 per cent of the time, compared with a 65 per cent Republican vote for Nixon in 1974. Democrats in 1974 voted with Ford 41 per cent of the time, compared with 46 per cent for Nixon in the same year.

202

ing back images of a world leader. He was gathering in all the rewards of being President, including designation as one of the "Best Dressed Men in America"—it was surely the first time that award had gone to a man who wore a belt with a big "M" buckle stamped "Go Blue" for the University of Michigan. Most important to the men in the White House concerned with the 1976 election, Ford's poll ratings were rising. The Harris poll in June 1975 reported for the first time that the President would defeat any of his probable Democratic opponents if an election were held then.

It was true that nobody seemed particularly angry with Jerry Ford, which was the idea of his whole life. The mood of the country—a euphemism for a reporter's personal impressions augmented by the opinions of a couple of cabdrivers —seemed to be a kind of dull hostility to government, politics and authority in general. It was possible that by diligently seeking to offend no one, American leaders had vaguely offended everyone, but there was a question of which was dominant, dullness or hostility.

Dullness. Unfocused offense. Comfortable mediocrity. Television. McDonald's. The least objectionable alternative. The maximum political energy the nation seemed capable of after the ravages of Watergate and Vietnam was a majority decision to stay home on Election Day 1974—fewer Americans were registering to vote, and more than half of those registered did not vote on November 5, 1974.

Perhaps it was destined to come to inertia and to a Ford in the White House. When Alexis de Tocqueville came in 1831 to see this mysterious thing, this new, energetic, democratic United States of America, he left believing that we and the leaders we produced would come to a comfortable end, losing not our democracy, but our energy.

"I am convinced," he wrote in *Democracy in America,* "that the intellectual anarchy which we see around us is not, as some suppose, the natural state for democracies. I think we should rather see it as an accidental characteristic peculiar to their youth . . . Men's main opinions become alike as the conditions of their lives become alike . . . It must, I think, be rare in a democracy for a man to suddenly conceive a system of ideas far different from those accepted by his contemporaries; and I suppose that, even should such an innovator arise, he would have great difficulty in making himself heard to begin with, and even more in convincing people.

"Thus, in proportion as men become more alike, and the principal of equality is more peaceably and deeply infused into the institutions and manners of the country, the rules for advancement become more inflexible, advancement itself slower, the difficulty of arriving quickly at a certain height far greater. From hatred of privilege and from the embarrassment of choosing, all men are at last constrained, whatever may be their standard, to pass the same ordeal; all are indiscriminately subjected to a multitude of petty preliminary exercises, in which their youth is wasted and their imagination quenched, so that they despair of ever fully attaining what is held out to them; and when at length they are in a condition to perform any extraordinary acts, the taste for such things has forsaken them.

"I confess that I apprehend much less for democratic society from the boldness than from the mediocrity of desires. What appears to me most to be dreaded is that in the midst of the small, incessant occupations of private life, ambition should lose its vigor and its greatness; that the passions of man should abate, but at the ame time be lowered; so that the march of society should every day become more tranquil and less aspiring."

If Tocqueville was right, and he's the best who ever worked my beat, then Gerald Ford, the thirty-eighth President of the United States, is not an accident or an anachronism, not some chummy caretaker who stumbled into our highest office. Gerald Ford is the future.

Index

decisiveness, 117, 124, 137, 149
dislike of confrontation, 7–8, 18, 139
economic views, 153–66, 173
emergence as major factor in American government, 5–8
enthusiasm for campaigning, 13–14, 44–45, 167–82
evaluation of first hundred days, 184–91, 197–204
folksiness, 67–68
generosity, 116–130
grasp of economic principles, 163–66
grasp of foreign policy, 47, 130, 132–33, 174
grasp of Presidential role, 66, 127, 132–33, 157, 160, 162–63, 174, 181
honesty, 40, 116
House Minority leadership, 6–7, 26–32, 46, 53–54, 103–04
House Republican Conference chairmanship, 5–6
instinct for direct response, 103
intellect, 25–27, 40, 41, 54, 66, 75, 81, 93, 116, 117, 120, 130, 133, 165, 188–91
knowledge gaps, 116–17, 119–20, 163, 188
legislative win record, 202n
loyalty, 7, 27–32, 41, 44, 52, 54–56, 116, 183
motivation for pardoning Nixon, 113–14, 117
"nice guy" qualities, 8, 9, 16, 18, 41, 66, 75, 103–04, 115–16, 191, 200
occupations previous to politics, 15
"openness and candor," 29, 32–33, 44, 57–58, 66, 84, 97, 100, 116, 126, 137, 155–59, 164, 184
personal popularity, 25–26, 28, 31, 68, 72
political style, 17–18, 23–34, 43–46, 107–11, 198–204
popularity as President, 63, 66–92, 107, 183–84, 197, 198, 203
public relations awareness, 7, 30, 41, 44n, 48–49, 65–67, 69, 83,

92–93, 97, 100, 103–04, 158, 173
reading habits, 121
relations with Nixon, 32–33, 39–42, 53, 57, 115
religious sentiments, 110, 113–14
reluctance to assert authority, 72–77, 80–81, 96, 122, 128, 165–66, 176, 177, 200
schooling, 14–15, 26
self-confidence, 116
speaking ability, 173, 176
stubbornness, 117, 118–19, 137
unpretentiousness, 68
vanity, 117–18
veto record, 118–19
Vice-Presidency, 30, 32, 39–42, 45–49, 53, 67, 103–04
warmth, 116
Watergate cover-up involvement, 51–54
Young Turks membership, 5–7
Ford, Gerald R., Sr., 114
Ford, Henry, II, 157
Ford, Michael, 58
Ford Motor Company, 27, 154
Franck, Thomas M., 92n
Freedom of Information Act, 118
Fresno, Ford's visit to, 176
Friedman, Milton (economist), 155
Friedman, Milton (speech writer), 159
Frucher, Sandy, 13
Future Farmers of America, 161

Galbraith, John Kenneth, 155
Gallegos, Bert, 81–82n
Gallup poll, 69, 92
Garn, Jake, 178
gasoline taxes, Ford's attitude toward, 117, 118, 137, 140
General Motors, 27, 155, 185
G.I. Bill, Ford's stand on, 179
Gibson, Andrew, 139–40
Giscard d'Estaing, Valéry, 133
Goebel, Paul, Jr., 173, 183
Goldberg, Arthur, 13
Goldwater, Barry, 6, 8, 26, 138, 148
Goodell, Charles
  formation of Young Turks, 5–7, 11

207

209

210

211